Praise for Arundhati Roy's essays

The scale of what Roy surveys is staggering. Her pointed indictment of India's hydroelectric industry—which has very little to show for the destruction it has wrought—is devastating.

—*New York Times Book Review*

Arundhati Roy combines brilliant reportage with a passionate, no-holds-barred commentary. I salute both her courage and her skill.

—Salman Rushdie

If [Roy] continues to upset the globalization applecart like a Tom Paine pamphleteer, she will either be greatly honored or thrown in jail.

—Paul Hawken, *Wired Magazine*

The millions of readers who enjoyed *The God of Small Things* will find the same poetry and grace informing her [essays].

—Barnes & Noble.com

Arundhati Roy's essays evoke a stark image of two Indias being driven "resolutely in opposite directions," a small India on its way to a "glittering destination" while the rest "melts into the darkness and disappears"—a microcosm of much of the world, she observes, though "in India your face is slammed right up against it." Traced with sensitivity and skill, the unfolding picture is interlaced with provocative reflections on the writer's mission and burden, and inspiring accounts of the "spectacular struggles" of popular movements that "refuse to lie down and die." Another impressive work by a fine writer.

—Noam Chomsky

Writers have proved when they turn their back to power and start to feel the pulse and pain of society, they become powerful. This is the power beyond power that Arundhati Roy brings forth in *Power Politics*.

—Vandana Shiva

Arundhati Roy combines her brilliant style as a novelist with her powerful commitment to social justice in producing these eloquent, penetrating essays.

—Howard Zinn

WAR TALK

ARUNDHATI ROY

SOUTH END PRESS
CAMBRIDGE, MASSACHUSETTS

First edition. Printed in Canada.

Library of Congress Cataloging-in-Publication Data

Roy, Arundhati
    War talk / Arundhati Roy.
        p. cm.
    Includes bibliographical references and index.
    ISBN 0-89308-723-9 (cloth) — ISBN 0-89608-724-7 (paper : alk. paper)
    1. World politics— 1989- 2. Nuclear weapons—India. 3. Nuclear weapons—Pakistan. 4. International relations. 5. Middle East—Politics and government—20th century. 6. Intervention (International law) 7. United States—Military policy. 8. Low intensity conflicts (Military science) I. Title.

D860.R69 2003
327.1'09'051—dc21

                                   2003042376

South End Press, 7 Brookline Street, #1
Cambridge, MA 02139-4146
www.southendpress.org

09 08 07 06 05 04 03   4 5 6 7

CONTENTS

WAR TALK: SUMMER GAMES WITH NUCLEAR BOMBS

When India and Pakistan conducted their nuclear tests in 1998, even those of us who condemned them balked at the hypocrisy of Western nuclear powers. Implicit in their denunciation of the tests was the notion that Blacks cannot be trusted with the Bomb. Now we are presented with the spectacle of our governments competing to confirm that belief.

As diplomats' families and tourists disappear from the subcontinent, Western journalists arrive in Delhi in droves. Many call me. "Why haven't you left the city?" they ask. "Isn't nuclear war a real possibility? Isn't Delhi a prime target?"

First appeared in *Frontline* magazine (India), Volume 19, Issue 12, June 8–21, 2002.

If nuclear weapons exist, then nuclear war is a real possibility. And Delhi is a prime target. It is.

But where shall we go? Is it possible to go out and buy another life because this one's not panning out?

If I go away, and everything and everyone—every friend, every tree, every home, every dog, squirrel, and bird that I have known and loved—is incinerated, how shall I live on? Whom shall I love? And who will love me back? Which society will welcome me and allow me to be the hooligan that I am here, at home?

So we're all staying. We huddle together. We realize how much we love each other. And we think, what a shame it would be to die now. Life's normal only because the macabre has become normal. While we wait for rain, for football, for justice, the old generals and eager boy-anchors on TV talk of first-strike and second-strike capabilities as though they're discussing a family board game.

My friends and I discuss *Prophecy*, the documentary about the bombing of Hiroshima and Nagasaki.[1] The fireball. The dead bodies choking the river. The living stripped of skin and hair. The singed, bald children, still alive, their clothes burned into their bodies. The thick, black, toxic water. The scorched, burning air. The cancers, implanted genetically, a malignant letter to the unborn. We remember especially the man who just melted into the steps of a building. We imagine ourselves like that. As stains on staircases. I imagine future generations of hushed schoolchildren pointing at my stain… That was a writer. Not she or he. *That.*

I'm sorry if my thoughts are stray and disconnected, not always worthy. Often ridiculous.

I think of a little mixed-breed dog I know. Each of his toes is a different color. Will he become a radioactive stain on a staircase too? My husband's writing a book on trees. He has a section on how figs are pollinated. Each fig only by its own specialized fig wasp. There are nearly a thousand different species of fig wasps, each a precise, exquisite synchrony, the product of millions of years of evolution.

All the fig wasps will be nuked. Zzzz. Ash. And my husband. And his book.

A dear friend, who's an activist in the anti-dam movement in the Narmada valley, is on indefinite hunger strike. Today is the fourteenth day of her fast. She and the others fasting with her are weakening quickly. They're protesting because the Madhya Pradesh government is bulldozing schools, clear-felling forests, uprooting hand pumps, forcing people from their villages to make way for the Maan Dam. The people have nowhere to go. And so, the hunger strike.[2]

What an act of faith and hope! How brave it is to believe that in today's world, reasoned, nonviolent protest will register, will matter. But will it? To governments that are comfortable with the notion of a wasted world, what's a wasted valley?

The threshold of horror has been ratcheted up so high that nothing short of genocide or the prospect of nuclear war merits mention. Peaceful resistance is treated with contempt. Terrorism's the real thing. The underlying principle of the War Against Terror, the very notion that war is an acceptable solution to terrorism, has ensured that terrorists in the subcontinent now have the power to trigger a nuclear war.

Displacement, dispossession, starvation, poverty, disease—these are now just the funnies, the comic-strip items. Our Home Minister says that Nobel laureate Amartya Sen has it all wrong—the key to India's development is not education and health but defense (and don't forget the kickbacks, O Best Beloved).[3]

Perhaps what he really meant was that war is the key to distracting the world's attention from fascism and genocide. To avoid dealing with any single issue of real governance that urgently needs to be addressed.

For the governments of India and Pakistan, Kashmir is not a *problem*, it's their perennial and spectacularly successful *solution*. Kashmir is the rabbit they pull out of their hats every time they need a rabbit. Unfortunately, it's a radioactive rabbit now, and it's careening out of control.

No doubt there is Pakistan-sponsored cross-border terrorism in Kashmir. But there are other kinds of terror in the valley. There's the inchoate nexus between jihadist militants, ex-militants, foreign mercenaries, local mercenaries, underworld Mafiosi, security forces, arms dealers, and criminalized politicians and officials on both sides of the border. There's also rigged elections, daily humiliation, "disappearances," and staged "encounters."[4]

And now the cry has gone up in the heartland: India is a Hindu country. Muslims can be murdered under the benign gaze of the state. Mass murderers will not be brought to justice. Indeed, they will stand for elections. Is

India to be a Hindu nation in the heartland and a secular one around the edges?

Meanwhile the International Coalition Against Terror makes war and preaches restraint. While India and Pakistan bay for each other's blood, the coalition is quietly laying gas pipelines, selling us weapons, and pushing through their business deals. (Buy now, pay later.) Britain, for example, is busy arming both sides.[5] Tony Blair's "peace" mission a few months ago was actually a business trip to discuss a one-billion pound deal (and don't forget the kickbacks, O Best Beloved) to sell sixty-six Hawk fighter-bombers to India.[6] Roughly, for the price of a *single* Hawk bomber, the government could provide one and a half million people with clean drinking water for life.[7]

"Why isn't there a peace movement?" Western journalists ask me ingenuously. How can there be a peace movement when, for most people in India, peace means a daily battle: for food, for water, for shelter, for dignity? War, on the other hand, is something professional soldiers fight far away on the border. And nuclear war—well, that's completely outside the realm of most people's comprehension. No one knows what a nuclear bomb is. No one cares to explain. As the Home Minister said, education is not a pressing priority.

The last question every visiting journalist always asks me is: Are you writing another book? That question mocks me. Another book? Right *now?* This talk of nuclear war displays such contempt for music, art, literature, and everything else that defines civilization. So what kind of book should I write?

It's not just the one million soldiers on the border who are living on hair-trigger alert. It's all of us. That's what nuclear bombs do. Whether they're used or not, they violate everything that is humane. They alter the meaning of life itself.

Why do we tolerate them? Why do we tolerate the men who use nuclear weapons to blackmail the entire human race?

AHIMSA

(NONVIOLENT RESISTANCE)

While the rest of us are mesmerized by talk of war and terrorism and wars against terror, in the state of Madhya Pradesh in central India, a little liferaft has set sail into the wind. On a pavement in Bhopal, in an area called Tin Shed, a small group of people has embarked on a journey of faith and hope. There's nothing new in what they're doing. What's new is the climate in which they're doing it.

Today is the twenty-ninth day of the indefinite hunger strike by four activists of the Narmada Bachao

First published in the *Hindustan Times* (India), June 12, 2002. This version is based on the version published in the *Christian Science Monitor* on July 5, 2002, as "Listen to the Nonviolent Poor: Allow for Peaceful Change, Before Violent Change Becomes Inevitable."

Andolan (NBA), the Save the Narmada Movement.[8] They have fasted two days longer than Gandhi did on any of his fasts during the freedom struggle. Their demands are more modest than his ever were. They are protesting against the Madhya Pradesh government's forcible eviction of more than one thousand Adivasi (indigenous) families to make way for the Maan Dam. All they're asking is that the government of Madhya Pradesh implement its own policy of providing land to those being displaced by the Maan Dam.

There's no controversy here. The dam has been built. The displaced people must be resettled before the reservoir fills up in the monsoon and submerges their villages. The four activists on fast are Vinod Patwa, who was one of the one hundred and fourteen thousand people displaced in 1990 by the Bargi Dam (which now, twelve years later, irrigates less land than it submerged); Mangat Verma, who will be displaced by the Maheshwar Dam if it is ever completed; Chittaroopa Palit, who has worked with the NBA for almost fifteen years; and twenty-two-year-old Ram Kunwar, the youngest and frailest of the activists. Hers is the first village that will be submerged when the waters rise in the Maan reservoir. In the weeks since she began her fast, Ram Kunwar has lost twenty pounds—almost one-fourth of her original body weight.

Unlike the other large dams such as the Sardar Sarovar, Maheshwar, and Indira Sagar, where the resettlement of hundreds of thousands of displaced people is simply not possible (except on paper, in court documents), in the case of Maan the total number of displaced people is about six thousand. People have even identified land that is available and could be bought and allotted to them by the government. And yet the government refuses.

Instead it's busy distributing paltry cash compensation, which is illegal and violates its own policy. It says quite openly that if it were to give in to the demands of the Maan "oustees" (that is, if it implemented its own policy), it would set a precedent for the hundreds of thousands of people, most of them Dalits (untouchables) and Adivasis, who are slated to be submerged (without rehabilitation) by the twenty-nine other big dams planned in the Narmada valley. And the state government's commitment to these projects remains absolute, regardless of the social and environmental costs.

As Vinod, Mangat, Chittaroopa, and Ram Kunwar gradually weaken, as their systems close down and the risk of irreversible organ failure and sudden death sets in, no government official has bothered to even pay them a visit.

Let me tell you a secret—it's not all unwavering resolve and steely determination on the burning pavement under the pitiless sun at Tin Shed. The jokes about slimming and weight loss are becoming a little poignant now. There are tears of anger and frustration. There is trepidation and real fear. But underneath all that, there's pure grit.

What will happen to them? Will they just go down in the ledgers as "the price of progress"? That phrase cleverly frames the whole argument as one between those who are pro-development versus those who are anti-development—and suggests the inevitability of the choice you have to make: pro-development, what else? It slyly suggests that movements like the NBA are antiquated and absurdly anti-electricity or anti-irrigation. This of course is nonsense.

The NBA believes that Big Dams are obsolete. It believes there are more democratic, more local, more economically viable and environmentally sustainable ways of generating electricity and managing water systems. It is demanding *more* modernity, not less. It is demanding *more* democracy, not less. And look at what's happening instead.

War Talk

Even at the height of the war rhetoric, even as India and Pakistan threatened each other with nuclear annihilation, the question of reneging on the Indus Waters Treaty between the two countries did not arise.[9] Yet in Madhya Pradesh, the police and administration entered Adivasi villages with bulldozers. They sealed hand pumps, demolished school buildings, and clear-felled trees in order to force people from their homes. They *sealed* hand pumps. And so, the indefinite hunger strike.

Any government's condemnation of terrorism is only credible if it shows itself to be responsive to persistent, reasonable, closely argued, nonviolent dissent. And yet, what's happening is just the opposite. The world over, nonviolent resistance movements are being crushed and broken. If we do not respect and honor them, by default we privilege those who turn to violent means.

Across the world, when governments and the media lavish all their time, attention, funds, research, space, sophistication, and seriousness on war talk and terrorism, then the message that goes out is disturbing and dangerous: If you seek to air and redress a public grievance, violence is more effective than nonviolence. Unfortunately, if peaceful change is not given a chance, then violent change becomes inevitable. That violence will be (and already is) random, ugly, and unpredictable. What's happening in Kashmir, the northeastern states of India, and Andhra Pradesh is all part of this process.

Right now the NBA is not just fighting big dams. It's fighting for the survival of India's greatest gift to the world: nonviolent resistance. You could call it the Ahimsa Bachao Andolan (ahimsa means "nonviolent resistance"), or the Save Nonviolence Movement.

Over the years our government has shown nothing but contempt for the people of the Narmada valley. Contempt for their argument. Contempt for their movement.

In the twenty-first century the connection between religious fundamentalism, nuclear nationalism, and the pauperization of whole populations because of corporate globalization is becoming impossible to ignore. While the Madhya Pradesh government has categorically said it has no land for the rehabilitation of displaced people, reports say that it is preparing the ground (pardon the pun) to make huge tracts of land available for corporate agriculture. This in turn will set off another cycle of displacement and impoverishment.

War Talk

Can we prevail on Digvijay Singh—the secular, "green" chief minister of Madhya Pradesh—to substitute some of his public relations with a *real* change in policy? If he did, he would go down in history as a man of vision and true political courage.

If the Congress Party wishes to be taken seriously as an alternative to the destructive right-wing religious fundamentalists who have brought us to the threshold of ruin, it will have to do more than condemn communalism and participate in empty nationalist rhetoric. It will have to do some real work and some real listening to the people it claims to represent.

As for the rest of us, concerned citizens, peace activists, and the like—it's not enough to sing songs about giving peace a chance. Doing everything we can to support movements like the Narmada Bachao Andolan is *how* we give peace a chance. *This* is the real war against terror.

Go to Bhopal. Just ask for Tin Shed.[10]

DEMOCRACY: WHO IS SHE WHEN SHE IS AT HOME?

Last night a friend from Baroda called. Weeping. It took her fifteen minutes to tell me what the matter was. It wasn't very complicated. Only that a friend of hers, Sayeeda,[11] had been caught by a mob. Only that her stomach had been ripped open and stuffed with burning rags. Only that after she died someone carved "OM" on her forehead.[12]

Precisely which Hindu scripture preaches this?

Our Prime Minister, A.B. Vajpayee, justified this as part of the retaliation by outraged Hindus against Muslim "terrorists" who burned alive fifty-eight Hindu passen-

First published in the May 6, 2002, issue of *Outlook* magazine (India). A shorter version of this essay appeared under the title "Fascism's Firm Footprint in India" in *The Nation* magazine on September 30, 2002, and in Betsy Reed, ed., *Nothing Sacred: Women Respond to Religious Fundamentalism and Terror* (New York: Nation Books, 2002).

gers on the Sabarmati Express in Godhra.[13] Each of those who died that hideous death was someone's brother, someone's mother, someone's child. Of course they were.

Which particular verse in the Koran required that they be roasted alive?

The more the two sides try and call attention to their religious differences by slaughtering each other, the less there is to distinguish them from one another. They worship at the same altar. They're both apostles of the same murderous god, whoever he is. In an atmosphere so vitiated, for anybody, and in particular the Prime Minister, to arbitrarily decree exactly where the cycle started is malevolent and irresponsible.

Right now we're sipping from a poisoned chalice —a flawed democracy laced with religious fascism. Pure arsenic.

What shall we do? What *can* we do?

We have a ruling party that's hemorrhaging. Its rhetoric against terrorism, the passing of the Prevention of Terrorism Act (POTA), the saber-rattling against Pakistan (with the underlying nuclear threat), the massing of almost a million soldiers on the border on hair-trigger alert and, most dangerous of all, the attempt to communalize and falsify school history textbooks—none of this has prevented it from being humiliated in election after election.[14] Even its old party trick—the revival of the plans to replace the destroyed mosque in Ayodhya with the Ram Mandir—didn't quite work out.[15] Desperate now, it has turned for succor to the state of Gujarat.

Gujarat, the only major state in India to have a Bharatiya Janata Party (BJP) government, has, for some years, been the petri dish in which Hindu fascism has been fomenting an elaborate political experiment. In March 2002, the initial results were put on public display.

Within hours of the Godhra outrage, a meticulously planned pogrom was unleashed against the Muslim community. It was led from the front by the Hindu nationalist Vishwa Hindu Parishad (VHP) and the Bajrang Dal. Officially the number of dead is eight hundred. Independent reports put the figure as high as two thousand.[16] More than one hundred and fifty thousand people, driven from their homes, now live in refugee camps.[17] Women were stripped, gang-raped; parents were bludgeoned to death in front of their children.[18] Two hundred and forty dargahs and one hundred and eighty masjids were destroyed. In

Ahmedabad, the tomb of Wali Gujarati, the founder of the modern Urdu poem, was demolished and paved over in the course of a night.[19] The tomb of the musician Ustad Faiyaz Ali Khan was desecrated and wreathed in burning tires.[20] Arsonists burned and looted shops, homes, hotels, textiles mills, buses, and private cars. Tens of thousands have lost their jobs.[21]

A mob surrounded the house of former Congress MP Ehsan Jaffri. His phone calls to the Director General of Police, the Police Commissioner, the Chief Secretary, the Additional Chief Secretary (Home) were ignored. The mobile police vans around his house did not intervene. The mob dragged Ehsan Jaffri out of his house, and dismembered him.[22] Of course it's only a coincidence that Jaffri was a trenchant critic of Gujarat's Chief Minister, Narendra Modi, during his campaign for the Rajkot Assembly by-election in February.

Across Gujarat, thousands of people made up the mobs. They were armed with petrol bombs, guns, knives, swords, and tridents.[23] Apart from the VHP and Bajrang Dal's usual lumpen constituency, there were Dalits and Adivasis who were brought in buses and trucks. Middle-class people participated in the looting.

(On one memorable occasion a family arrived in a Mitsubishi Lancer.[24]) There was a deliberate, systematic attempt to destroy the economic base of the Muslim community. The leaders of the mob had computer-generated cadastral lists marking out Muslim homes, shops, businesses, and even partnerships. They had mobile phones to coordinate the action. They had trucks loaded with thousands of gas cylinders, hoarded weeks in advance, which they used to blow up Muslim commercial establishments. They had not just police protection and police connivance but also covering fire.[25]

While Gujarat burned, our Prime Minister was on MTV promoting his new poems.[26] (Reports say cassettes have sold a hundred thousand copies.) It took him more than a month—and two vacations in the hills—to make it to Gujarat.[27] When he did, shadowed by the chilling Modi, he gave a speech at the Shah Alam refugee camp.[28] His mouth moved, he tried to express concern, but no real sound emerged except the mocking of the wind whistling through a burned, bloodied, broken world. Next we knew, he was bobbing around in a golf cart, striking business deals in Singapore.[29]

The killers still stalk Gujarat's streets. For weeks the lynch mob was the arbiter of the routine affairs of daily life: who can live where, who can say what, who can meet whom, and where and when. Its mandate expanded from religious affairs, to property disputes, family altercations, the planning and allocation of water resources…(which is why Medha Patkar of the Narmada Bachao Andolan was assaulted).[30] Muslim businesses have been shut down. Muslim people are not served in restaurants. Muslim children are not welcome in schools. Muslim students are too terrified to sit for their exams.[31] Muslim parents live in dread that their infants might forget what they've been told and give themselves away by saying "Ammi!" or "Abba!" in public and invite sudden and violent death.

Notice has been given: *this is just the beginning.*

Is this the Hindu Rashtra, the Nation that we've all been asked to look forward to? Once the Muslims have been "shown their place," will milk and Coca-Cola flow across the land? Once the Ram Mandir is built, will there be a shirt on every back and a roti in every belly?[32] Will every tear be wiped from every eye? Can we expect an anniversary celebration next year? Or will there be someone else to hate by then? Alphabetically: Adivasis, Buddhists,

Christians, Dalits, Parsis, Sikhs? Those who wear jeans or speak English or those who have thick lips or curly hair? We won't have to wait long. It's started already. Will the established rituals continue? Will people be beheaded, dismembered, and urinated upon? Will fetuses be ripped from their mothers' wombs and slaughtered? (What kind of depraved vision can even *imagine* India without the range and beauty and spectacular anarchy of all these cultures? India would become a tomb and smell like a crematorium.)

No matter who they were, or how they were killed, each person who died in Gujarat in the weeks gone by deserves to be mourned. There have been hundreds of outraged letters to journals and newspapers asking why the "pseudo-secularists" do not condemn the burning of the Sabarmati Express in Godhra with the same degree of outrage with which they condemn the killings in the rest of Gujarat. What they don't seem to understand is that there *is* a fundamental difference between a pogrom such as the one taking place in Gujarat now and the burning of the Sabarmati Express in Godhra. We still don't know who exactly was responsible for the carnage in Godhra.[33] Whoever did it—whatever their political or religious per-

suasion—committed a terrible crime. But every independent report says the pogrom against the Muslim
community in Gujarat—billed by the government as a
spontaneous "reaction"—has at best been conducted under the benign gaze of the state and, at worst, with active
state collusion.[34] Either way, the state is criminally culpable.
And the state acts in the name of its citizens. So, as a citizen, I am forced to acknowledge that I am somehow made
complicit in the Gujarat pogrom. It is this that outrages me.
And it is this that puts a completely different complexion
on the two massacres.

After the Gujarat massacres, at its convention in
Bangalore, the Rashtriya Swayamsevak Sangh (RSS), the
moral and cultural guild of the BJP, of which the Prime
Minister, the Home Minister, and Chief Minister Modi
himself are all members, called upon Muslims to earn the
"goodwill" of the majority community.[35] At the meeting of
the national executive of the BJP in Goa, Narendra Modi
was greeted as a hero. His smirking offer to resign from the
Chief Minister's post was unanimously turned down.[36] In a
recent public speech he compared the events of the last
few weeks in Gujarat to Gandhi's Dandi March—both,

according to him, significant moments in the Struggle for Freedom.

While the parallels between contemporary India and pre-war Germany are chilling, they're not surprising. (The founders of the RSS have, in their writings, been frank in their admiration for Hitler and his methods.[37]) One difference is that here in India we don't have a Hitler. We have, instead, a travelling extravaganza, a mobile symphonic orchestra. The hydra-headed, many-armed Sangh Parivar—the "joint family" of Hindu political and cultural organizations—with the BJP, the RSS, the VHP, and the Bajrang Dal, each playing a different instrument. Its utter genius lies in its apparent ability to be all things to all people at all times.

The Parivar has an appropriate head for every occasion. An old versifier with rhetoric for every season. A rabble-rousing hardliner, Lal Krishna Advani, for Home Affairs; a suave one, Jaswant Singh, for Foreign Affairs; a smooth, English-speaking lawyer, Arun Jaitley, to handle TV debates; a cold-blooded creature, Narendra Modi, for a Chief Minister; and the Bajrang Dal and the VHP, grassroots workers in charge of the physical labor that goes into the business of genocide. Finally, this many-headed extravaganza has a lizard's tail which drops off when it's in trouble and grows back again: a specious socialist dressed up as Defense Minister, who it sends on its damage-limitation missions—wars, cyclones, genocides. They trust him to press the right buttons, hit the right note.

The Sangh Parivar speaks in as many tongues as a whole corsage of tridents. It can say several contradictory things simultaneously. While one of its heads (the VHP) exhorts millions of its cadres to prepare for the Final Solution, its titular head (the Prime Minister) assures the nation that all citizens, regardless of their religion, will be treated equally. It can ban books and films and burn paintings for "insulting Indian culture." Simultaneously, it can mortgage the equivalent of sixty percent of the entire country's rural development budget as profit to Enron.[38] It contains within itself the full spectrum of political opinion, so what would normally be a public fight between two adversarial political parties is now just a family matter. However acrimonious the quarrel, it's *always* conducted in public, always resolved amicably, and the audience always goes away satisfied it's got value for its money—anger, action, revenge, intrigue, remorse, poetry, and plenty of gore. It's our own vernacular version of Full Spectrum Dominance.[39]

But when the chips are down, *really* down, the squabbling heads quiet, and it becomes chillingly apparent that underneath all the clamor and the noise, a single heart beats. And an unforgiving mind with saffron-saturated tunnel vision works overtime.

There have been pogroms in India before, every kind of pogrom—directed at particular castes, tribes, religious faiths. In 1984, following the assassination of Indira Gandhi, the Congress Party presided over the massacre of three thousand Sikhs in Delhi, every bit as macabre as the one in Gujarat.[40] At the time, Rajiv Gandhi, never known for an elegant turn of phrase, said, "When a large tree falls, the earth shakes."[41] In 1985, the Congress swept the polls. On a *sympathy* wave! Eighteen years have gone by, and almost no one has been punished.

Take any politically volatile issue—the nuclear tests, the Babri Masjid, the Tehelka scam, the stirring of the communal cauldron for electoral advantage—and you'll see the Congress Party has been there before. In every case, the Congress sowed the seed and the BJP has swept in to reap the hideous harvest. So in the event that we're called upon to vote, *is* there a difference between the two? The answer is a faltering but distinct "yes." Here's why: It's true that the Congress Party has sinned, and grievously, and for decades together. But it has done by night what the BJP does by day. It has done covertly, stealthily, hypocritically, shamefacedly what the BJP does with pride. And this is an important difference.

Whipping up communal hatred is part of the mandate of the Sangh Parivar. It has been planned for *years*. It has been injecting a slow-release poison directly into civil society's bloodstream. Hundreds of RSS shakhas and Saraswati shishu mandirs across the country have been indoctrinating thousands of children and young people, stunting their minds with religious hatred and falsified history, including unfactual or wildly exaggerated accounts of the rape and pillaging of Hindu women and Hindu temples by Muslim rulers in the precolonial period. They're no different from, and no less dangerous than, the madrassas all over Pakistan and Afghanistan which spawned the Taliban. In states like Gujarat, the police, the administration, and the political cadres at every level have been systematically penetrated.[42] The whole enterprise has huge popular appeal, which it would be foolish to underestimate or misunderstand. It has a formidable religious, ideological, political, and administrative underpinning. This kind of power, this kind of reach, can only be achieved with state backing.

Some madrassas, the Muslim equivalent of hothouses cultivating religious hatred, try and make up in frenzy and foreign funding what they lack in state support. They provide the perfect foil for Hindu communalists to dance their dance of mass paranoia and hatred. (In fact, they serve that purpose so perfectly they might just as well be working as a team.)

Under this relentless pressure, what will most likely happen is that the majority of the Muslim community will resign itself to living in ghettos as second-class citizens, in constant fear, with no civil rights and no recourse to justice. What will daily life be like for them? Any little thing, an altercation in a cinema queue or a fracas at a traffic light, could turn lethal. So they will learn to keep very quiet, to accept their lot, to creep around the edges of the society in which they live. Their fear will transmit itself to other minorities. Many, particularly the young, will probably turn to militancy. They will do terrible things. Civil society will be called upon to condemn them. Then

President Bush's canon will come back to us: "Either you are with us or you are with the terrorists."[43]

Those words hang frozen in time like icicles. For years to come, butchers and genocidists will fit their grisly mouths around them ("lip-synch," filmmakers call it) in order to justify their butchery.

Bal Thackeray of the Shiv Sena, who has lately been feeling a little upstaged by Modi, has the lasting solution. He's called for civil war. Isn't that just perfect? Then Pakistan won't need to bomb us, we can bomb ourselves. Let's turn all of India into Kashmir. Or Bosnia. Or Palestine. Or Rwanda. Let's all suffer forever. Let's buy expensive guns and explosives to kill each other with. Let the British arms dealers and the American weapons manufacturers grow fat on our spilled blood.[44] We could ask the Carlyle group—of which the Bush and bin Laden families were both shareholders—for a bulk discount.[45] Maybe if things go really well, we'll become like Afghanistan. (And look at the publicity they've gone and got themselves.) When all our farmlands are mined, our buildings destroyed, our infrastructure reduced to rubble, our children physically maimed and mentally wrecked, when we've nearly wiped ourselves out with self-manufactured hatred, maybe we can appeal to the Americans to help us out. Air-dropped airline meals, anyone?

How close we have come to self-destruction! Another step and we'll be in free fall. And yet the government presses on. At the Goa meeting of the BJP's national executive, the Prime Minister of secular, democratic India, A.B. Vajpayee, made history. He became the first Indian Prime Minister to cross the threshold and publicly unveil an unconscionable bigotry against Muslims, which even George Bush and Donald Rumsfeld would be embarrassed to own up to. "Wherever Muslims are," he said, "they do not want to live peacefully."[46]

Shame on him. But if only it were just him: In the immediate aftermath of the Gujarat holocaust, confident of the success of its "experiment," the BJP wants a snap poll. "The *gentlest* of people," my friend from Baroda said to me, "the *gentlest* of people, in the gentlest of voices, says 'Modi is our hero.'"

Some of us nurtured the naive hope that the magnitude of the horror of the last few weeks would make the secular parties, however self-serving, unite in sheer outrage. On its own, the BJP does not have the mandate of the people of India. It does not have the mandate to push through the Hindutva project. We hoped that the twenty-two allies that make up the BJP-led coalition would withdraw their support. We thought, quite stupidly, that they would see that there could be no bigger test of their moral fiber, of their commitment to their avowed principles of secularism.

It's a sign of the times that not a single one of the BJP's allies has withdrawn support. In every shifty eye you see that faraway look of someone doing mental math to calculate which constituencies and portfolios they'll retain and which ones they'll lose if they pull out. Deepak Parekh is one of the only CEOs of India's corporate community to condemn what happened.[47] Farooq Abdullah, Chief Minister of Jammu and Kashmir and the only prominent Muslim politician left in India, is currying favor with the government by supporting Modi because he nurses the dim hope that he might become Vice President of India very soon.[48] And worst of all, Mayawati, leader of the Bahujan Samaj Party (BSP), the People's Socialist Party, the great hope of the lower castes, has forged an alliance with the BJP in Uttar Pradesh.[49]

The Congress and the Left parties have launched a public agitation asking for Modi's resignation.[50] *Resignation?* Have we lost all sense of proportion? Criminals are not meant to *resign*. They're meant to be charged, tried, and convicted. As those who burned the train in Godhra should be. As the mobs and those members of the police force and the administration who planned and participated in the pogrom in the rest of Gujarat should be. As those responsible for raising the pitch of the frenzy to boiling point must be. The Supreme Court has the option of acting against Modi and the Bajrang Dal and the VHP. There are hundreds of testimonies. There are masses of evidence.

But in India if you are a butcher or a genocidist who happens to be a politician, you have every reason to be optimistic. No one even *expects* politicians to be prosecuted. To demand that Modi and his henchmen be arraigned and put away would make other politicians vulnerable to their own unsavory pasts. So instead they disrupt Parliament, shout a lot. Eventually those in power set up commissions of inquiry, ignore the findings, and between themselves makes sure the juggernaut chugs on.

Already the issue has begun to morph. Should elections be allowed or not? Should the Election Commission decide that? Or the Supreme Court? Either way, whether elections are held or deferred, by allowing Modi to walk free, by allowing him to continue with his career as a politician, the fundamental, governing principles of democracy are not just being subverted but deliberately sabotaged. This kind of democracy is the *problem,* not the solution. Our society's greatest strength is being turned into her deadliest enemy. What's the point of us all going on about "deepening democracy," when it's being bent and twisted into something unrecognizable?

What if the BJP *does* win the elections? After all, George Bush had a sixty percent rating in his War Against Terror, and Ariel Sharon has an even stronger mandate for his bestial invasion of Palestine.[51] Does that make everything all right? Why not dispense with the legal system, the constitution, the press—the whole shebang—morality *itself,* why not chuck it and put everything up for a vote? Genocides can become the subject of opinion polls and massacres can have marketing campaigns.

Fascism's firm footprint has appeared in India. Let's mark the date: Spring 2002. While we can thank the American President and the Coalition Against Terror for creating a congenial international atmosphere for fascism's ghastly debut, we cannot credit them for the years it has been brewing in our public and private lives.

War Talk

It breezed in after the Pokhran nuclear tests in 1998.[52]
From then onwards, the massed energy of bloodthirsty
patriotism became openly acceptable political currency.
The "weapons of peace" trapped India and Pakistan in a
spiral of brinkmanship—threat and counter-threat, taunt
and counter-taunt.[53] And now, one war and hundreds of
dead later,[54] more than a million soldiers from both armies are massed at the border, eyeball to eyeball, locked in
a pointless nuclear standoff. The escalating belligerence
against Pakistan has ricocheted off the border and entered our own body politic, like a sharp blade slicing
through the vestiges of communal harmony and toler-
ance between the Hindu and Muslim communities. In no
time at all, the godsquadders from hell have colonized the
public imagination. And we allowed them in. Each time
the hostility between India and Pakistan is cranked up,
within India there's a corresponding increase in the hostility toward the Muslims. With each battle cry against Pakistan, we inflict a wound on ourselves, on our way of life,
on our spectacularly diverse and ancient civilization, on
everything that makes India different from Pakistan. In-
creasingly, Indian nationalism has come to mean Hindu
nationalism, which defines itself not through a respect or

regard for itself, but through a hatred of the Other. And the Other, for the moment, is not just Pakistan, it's Muslims. It's disturbing to see how neatly nationalism dovetails into fascism. While we must not allow the fascists to define what the nation is, or who it belongs to, it's worth keeping in mind that nationalism—in all its many avatars: communist, capitalist, and fascist—has been at the root of almost all the genocide of the twentieth century. On the issue of nationalism, it's wise to proceed with caution.

Can we not find it in ourselves to belong to an ancient civilization instead of to just a recent nation? To love a *land* instead of just patrolling a territory? The Sangh Parivar understands nothing of what civilization means. It seeks to limit, reduce, define, dismember, and desecrate the memory of what we were, our understanding of what we are, and our dreams of who we want to be. What kind of India do they want? A limbless, headless, soulless torso, left bleeding under the butcher's cleaver with a flag driven deep into her mutilated heart? Can we let that happen? Have we let it happen?

The incipient, creeping fascism of the past few years has been groomed by many of our "democratic" institutions. Everyone has flirted with it—Parliament, the press, the police, the administration, the public. Even "secularists" have been guilty of helping to create the right climate. Each time you defend the right of an institution, *any* institution (including the Supreme Court), to exercise unfettered, unaccountable powers that must never be challenged, you move toward fascism. To be fair, perhaps not everyone recognized the early signs for what they were.

The national press has been startlingly courageous in its denunciation of the events of the last few weeks. Many of the BJP's fellow-travelers, who have journeyed with it to the brink, are now looking down the abyss into the hell that was once Gujarat and turning away in genuine dismay. But how hard and for how long will they fight? This is not going to be like a publicity campaign for an upcoming cricket season. And there will not always be spectacular carnage to report on. Fascism is also about the slow, steady infiltration of all the instruments of state power. It's about the slow erosion of civil liberties, about unspectacular day-to-day injustices. Fighting it means fighting to win back the minds and hearts of people. Fighting it does not mean asking for RSS shakhas and the madrassas that are overtly communal to be banned, it means working toward the day when they're voluntarily abandoned as bad ideas. It means keeping an eagle eye on public institutions and demanding accountability. It means putting your ear to the ground and listening to the whispering of the truly powerless. It means giving a forum to the myriad voices from the hundreds of resistance movements across the country which are speaking about *real* things—about bonded labor, marital rape, sexual preferences, women's wages, uranium dumping, unsustainable mining, weavers' woes, farmers' suicides. It means fighting displacement and dispossession and the relentless, everyday violence of abject poverty. Fighting it also means not allowing your newspaper columns and prime-time TV spots to be hijacked by their spurious passions and their staged theatrics, which are designed to divert attention from everything else.

While most people in India have been horrified by what happened in Gujarat, many thousands of the indoctrinated are preparing to journey deeper into the heart of the horror. Look around you and you'll see in little parks, in empty lots, in village commons, the RSS is marching, hoisting its saffron flag. Suddenly they're everywhere, grown men in khaki shorts marching, marching, marching. To *where?* For *what?* Their disregard for history shields them from the knowledge that fascism will thrive for a short while and then self-annihilate because of its inherent stupidity. But unfortunately, like the radioactive fallout of a nuclear strike, it has a half-life that will cripple generations to come.

These levels of rage and hatred cannot be contained, cannot be expected to subside, with public censure and denunciation. Hymns of brotherhood and love are great, but not enough.

Historically, fascist movements have been fuelled by feelings of national disillusionment. Fascism has come to India after the dreams that fuelled the Freedom Struggle have been frittered away like so much loose change.

Independence itself came to us as what Gandhi famously called a "wooden loaf"—a notional freedom tainted by the blood of the thousands who died during Partition.[55] For more than half a century now, the hatred and mutual distrust has been exacerbated, toyed with, and never allowed to heal by politicians, led from the front by Indira Gandhi. Every political party has tilled the marrow of our secular parliamentary democracy, mining it for electoral advantage. Like termites excavating a mound, they've made tunnels and underground passages, undermining the meaning of "secular," until it has become just an empty shell that's about to implode. Their tilling has weakened the foundations of the structure that connects the Constitution, Parliament, and the courts of law—the configuration of checks and balances that forms the backbone of a parliamentary democracy. Under the circumstances, it's futile to go on blaming politicians and demanding from them a morality of which they're incapable. There's something pitiable about a people that constantly bemoans its leaders. If they've let us down, it's only because we've allowed them to. It could be argued that civil society has failed its leaders as much as leaders have failed civil society. We have to accept that there is a dangerous, systemic flaw in our parliamentary democracy that politicians *will* exploit. And that's what results in the kind of conflagration that we have witnessed in Gujarat. There's fire in the ducts. We have to address this issue and come up with a *systemic* solution.

But politicians' exploitation of communal divides is by no means the only reason that fascism has arrived on our shores.

Over the past fifty years, ordinary citizens' modest hopes for lives of dignity, security, and relief from abject poverty have been systematically snuffed out. Every "democratic" institution in this country has shown itself to be unaccountable, inaccessible to the ordinary citizen, and either unwilling or incapable of acting in the interests of genuine social justice. *Every* strategy for real social change—land reform, education, public health, the equitable distribution of natural resources, the implementation of positive discrimination—has been cleverly, cunningly, and consistently scuttled and rendered ineffectual by those castes and that class of people which has a stranglehold on the political process. And now corporate globalization is being relentlessly and arbitrarily imposed on an essentially feudal society, tearing through its complex, tiered social fabric, ripping it apart culturally and economically.

There is very real grievance here. And the fascists didn't create it. But they have seized upon it, upturned it, and forged from it a hideous, bogus sense of pride. They have mobilized human beings using the lowest common denominator—religion. People who have lost control over their lives, people who have been uprooted from their homes and communities, who have lost their culture and their language, are being made to feel proud of *something*. Not something they have striven for and achieved, not something they can count as a personal accomplishment, but something they just happen to be. Or, more accurately, something they happen *not* to be. And the falseness, the emptiness, of that pride is fuelling a gladiatorial anger that is then directed toward a simulated target that has been wheeled into the amphitheater.

How else can you explain the project of trying to disenfranchise, drive out, or exterminate the second-poorest community in this country, using as your foot soldiers the very poorest (Dalits and Adivasis)? How else can you explain why Dalits in Gujarat, who have been despised, oppressed, and treated worse than refuse by the upper castes for thousands of years, have joined hands with their oppressors to turn on those who are only marginally less unfortunate than they themselves? Are they just wage slaves, mercenaries for hire? Is it all right to patronize them and absolve them of responsibility for their own actions? Or am I being obtuse? Perhaps it's common practice for the unfortunate to vent their rage and hatred on the *next* most unfortunate, because their *real* adversaries are inaccessible, seemingly invincible, and completely out of range. Because their own leaders have cut loose and are feasting at the high table, leaving them to wander rudderless in the wilderness, spouting nonsense about returning to the Hindu fold. (The first step, presumably, toward founding a global Hindu empire, as realistic a goal as fascism's previously failed projects—the restoration of Roman glory, the purification of the German race, or the establishment of an Islamic sultanate.)

One hundred and thirty million Muslims live in India.[56] Hindu fascists regard them as legitimate prey. Do people like Modi and Bal Thackeray think that the world will stand by and watch while they're liquidated in a "civil war"? Press reports say that the European Union and several other countries have condemned what happened in Gujarat and likened it to Nazi rule.[57] The Indian government's portentous response is that foreigners should not use the Indian media to comment on what is an "internal matter" (like the chilling goings-on in Kashmir?).[58] What next? Censorship? Closing down the Internet? Blocking international calls? Killing the wrong "terrorists" and fudging the DNA samples? There is no terrorism like state terrorism.

But who will take them on? Their fascist cant can perhaps be dented by some blood and thunder from the Opposition. So far only Laloo Yadav, head of the Rashtriya

Janata Dal (RJD), the National People's Party, in Bihar, has shown himself to be truly passionate: *"Kaun mai ka lal kehtha hai ki yeh Hindu Rashtra hai? Usko yahan bhej do, chhaahti phad doonga!"* (Which mother's son says this is a Hindu Nation? Send him here, I'll tear his chest open.)[59]

Unfortunately, there's no quick fix. Fascism itself can only be turned away if all those who are outraged by it show a commitment to social justice that equals the intensity of their indignation.

Are we ready to get off our starting blocks? Are we ready, many millions of us, to rally, not just on the streets, but at work and in schools and in our homes, in every decision we take, and every choice we make?

Or not just yet…?

If not, then years from now, when the rest of the world has shunned us (as it should), we too will learn, like the ordinary citizens of Hitler's Germany, to recognize revulsion in the gaze of our fellow human beings. We too will find ourselves unable to look our own children in the eye, for the shame of what we did and didn't do. For the shame of what we allowed to happen.

This is *us*. In *India*. Heaven help us make it through the night.

COME SEPTEMBER

Writers imagine that they cull stories from the world. I'm beginning to believe that vanity makes them think so. That it's actually the other way around. Stories cull writers from the world. Stories reveal themselves to us. The public narrative, the private narrative—they colonize us. They commission us. They insist on being told. Fiction and nonfiction are only different techniques of storytelling. For reasons I do not fully understand, fiction dances out of me. Nonfiction is wrenched out by the aching, broken world I wake up to every morning.

The theme of much of what I write, fiction as well as nonfiction, is the relationship between power and power-

First presented as a lecture in Santa Fe, New Mexico, at the Lensic Performing Arts Center, September 18, 2002. Sponsored by the Lannan Foundation: www.lannan.org.

lessness and the endless, circular conflict they're engaged in. John Berger, that most wonderful writer, once wrote:

> Never again will a single story be told as though
> it's the only one.[60]

There can never be a single story. There are only ways of seeing. So when I tell a story, I tell it not as an ideologue who wants to pit one absolutist ideology against another, but as a storyteller who wants to share her way of seeing. Though it might appear otherwise, my writing is not really about nations and histories, it's about power. About the paranoia and ruthlessness of power. About the physics of power. I believe that the accumulation of vast unfettered power by a state or a country, a corporation or an institution —or even an individual, a spouse, friend, or sibling— regardless of ideology, results in excesses such as the ones I will recount here.

Living as I do, as millions of us do, in the shadow of the nuclear holocaust that the governments of India and Pakistan keep promising their brainwashed citizenry, and in the global neighborhood of the War Against Terror (what President Bush rather biblically calls "the task that does not end"), I find myself thinking a great deal about the relationship between citizens and the state.[61]

In India, those of us who have expressed views on nuclear bombs, Big Dams, corporate globalization, and the rising threat of communal Hindu fascism—views that are at variance with the Indian government's—are branded "anti-national." While this accusation does not fill me with indignation, it's not an accurate description of what I do or how I think. An anti-national is a person who is against her own nation and, by inference, is pro some other one. But it isn't necessary to be anti-national to be deeply suspicious of all nationalism, to be anti-national*ism*. Nationalism of one kind or another was the cause of most of the genocide of the twentieth century. Flags are bits of colored cloth that governments use first to shrink-wrap people's minds and then as ceremonial shrouds to bury the dead. When independent, thinking people (and here I do not include the corporate media) begin to rally under flags, when writers, painters, musicians, film makers suspend their judgment and blindly yoke their art to the service of the nation, it's time for all of us to sit up and worry. In India we saw it happen soon after the nuclear tests in 1998 and during the Kargil War against Pakistan in 1999.

In the U.S. we saw it during the Gulf War and we see it now, during the War Against Terror. That blizzard of made-in-China American flags.[62]

Recently, those who have criticized the actions of the U.S. government (myself included) have been called "anti-American." Anti-Americanism is in the process of being consecrated into an ideology.

The term "anti-American" is usually used by the American establishment to discredit and—not falsely, but shall we say inaccurately—define its critics. Once someone is branded anti-American, the chances are that he or she will be judged before they're heard and the argument will be lost in the welter of bruised national pride.

What does the term "anti-American" *mean?* Does it mean you're anti-jazz? Or that you're opposed to free speech? That you don't delight in Toni Morrison or John Updike? That you have a quarrel with giant sequoias? Does it mean you don't admire the hundreds of thousands of American citizens who marched against nuclear weapons, or the thousands of war resisters who forced their government to withdraw from Vietnam? Does it mean that you hate all Americans?

War Talk

This sly conflation of America's culture, music, literature, the breathtaking physical beauty of the land, the ordinary pleasures of ordinary people with criticism of the
U.S. government's foreign policy (about which, thanks to
America's "free press," sadly, most Americans know very
little) is a deliberate and extremely effective strategy. It's
like a retreating army taking cover in a heavily populated
city, hoping that the prospect of hitting civilian targets will
deter enemy fire.

There are many Americans who would be mortified to
be associated with their government's policies. The most
scholarly, scathing, incisive, hilarious critiques of the hypocrisy and the contradictions in U.S. government policy
come from American citizens. When the rest of the world
wants to know what the U.S. government is up to, we turn
to Noam Chomsky, Edward Said, Howard Zinn, Ed
Herman, Amy Goodman, Michael Albert, Chalmers John-
son, William Blum, and Anthony Arnove to tell us what's
really going on.

Similarly, in India, not hundreds, but millions of us
would be ashamed and offended if we were in any way
implicated with the present Indian government's fascist
policies which, apart from the perpetration of state terror-

ism in the valley of Kashmir (in the name of fighting terrorism), have also turned a blind eye to the recent state-supervised pogrom against Muslims in Gujarat.[63] It would be absurd to think that those who criticize the Indian government are "anti-Indian"—although the government itself never hesitates to take that line. It is dangerous to cede to the Indian government or the American government or *anyone* for that matter, the right to define what "India" or "America" are, or ought to be.

To call someone anti-American, indeed, to *be* anti-American, (or for that matter anti-Indian, or anti-Timbuktuan) is not just racist, it's a failure of the imagination. An inability to see the world in terms other than those that the establishment has set out for you: If you're not a Bushie, you're a Taliban. If you don't love us, you hate us. If you're not Good, you're Evil. If you're not with us, you're with the terrorists.

Last year, like many others, I too made the mistake of scoffing at this post–September 11th rhetoric, dismissing it as foolish and arrogant. I've realized that it's not foolish at all. It's actually a canny recruitment drive for a misconceived, dangerous war. Every day I'm taken aback at how many people believe that opposing the war in Afghanistan amounts to supporting terrorism, or voting for the Taliban. Now that the initial aim of the war—capturing Osama bin Laden (dead or alive)—seems to have run into bad weather, the goalposts have been moved.[64] It's being made out that the whole point of the war was to topple the Taliban regime and liberate Afghan women from their burqas. We're being asked to believe that the U.S. marines are actually on a feminist mission. (If so, will their next stop be America's military ally Saudi Arabia?) Think of it this way: In India there are some pretty reprehensible social practices, against "untouchables," against Christians and Muslims, against women. Pakistan and Bangladesh have even worse ways of dealing with minority communities and women. Should they be bombed? Should Delhi, Islamabad, and Dhaka be destroyed? Is it possible to bomb bigotry out of India? Can we bomb our way to a feminist paradise? Is that how women won the vote in the United States? Or how slavery was abolished? Can we win redress for the genocide of the millions of Native Americans upon whose corpses the United States was founded by bombing Santa Fe?

None of us need anniversaries to remind us of what we cannot forget. So it is no more than coincidence that I happen to be here, on American soil, in September—this month of dreadful anniversaries. Uppermost on everybody's mind of course, particularly here in America, is the horror of what has come to be known as "9/11." Three thousand civilians lost their lives in that lethal terrorist strike.[65] The grief is still deep. The rage still sharp. The tears have not dried. And a strange, deadly war is raging around the world. Yet, each person who has lost a loved one surely knows secretly, deeply, that no war, no act of revenge, no daisy-cutters dropped on someone else's loved ones or someone else's children will blunt the edges of their pain or bring their own loved ones back. War cannot avenge those who have died. War is only a brutal desecration of their memory.

To fuel yet another war—this time against Iraq—by cynically manipulating people's grief, by packaging it for TV specials sponsored by corporations selling detergent or running shoes, is to cheapen and devalue grief, to drain it of meaning. What we are seeing now is a vulgar display of the *business* of grief, the commerce of grief, the pillaging of even the most private human feelings for political purpose. It is a terrible, violent thing for a state to do to its people.

War Talk

It's not a clever enough subject to speak of from a public platform, but what I would really love to talk to you about is loss. Loss and losing. Grief, failure, brokenness, numbness, uncertainty, fear, the death of feeling, the death of dreaming. The absolute, relentless, endless, habitual unfairness of the world. What does loss mean to individuals? What does it mean to whole cultures, whole peoples who have learned to live with it as a constant companion?

Since it is September 11th that we're talking about, perhaps it's in the fitness of things that we remember what that date means, not only to those who lost their loved ones in America last year, but to those in other parts of the world to whom that date has long held significance. This historical dredging is not offered as an accusation or a provocation. But just to share the grief of history. To thin the mist a little. To say to the citizens of America, in the gentlest, most human way: Welcome to the World.

Twenty-nine years ago, in Chile, on the 11th of September 1973, General Pinochet overthrew the democratically elected government of Salvador Allende in a CIA-backed coup. "I don't see why we need to stand by and watch a country go Communist due to the irresponsibility of its own people," said Henry Kissinger, Nobel Peace Laureate, then President Nixon's National Security Adviser.[66]

After the coup President Allende was found dead inside the presidential palace. Whether he was killed or whether he killed himself, we'll never know. In the regime of terror that ensued, thousands of people were killed. Many more simply "disappeared." Firing squads conducted public executions. Concentration camps and torture chambers were opened across the country. The dead were buried in mine shafts and unmarked graves. For more than sixteen years the people of Chile lived in dread of the midnight knock, of routine disappearances, of sudden arrest and torture.[67]

In 2000, following the 1998 arrest of General Pinochet in Britain, thousands of secret documents were declassified by the U.S. government.[68] They contain unequivocal evidence of the CIA's involvement in the coup as well as the fact that the U.S. government had detailed information about the situation in Chile during General Pinochet's reign. Yet Kissinger assured the general of his support: "In the United States, as you know, we are sympathetic with what you are trying to do," he said, "We wish your government well."[69]

Those of us who have only ever known life in a democracy, however flawed, would find it hard to imagine what living in a dictatorship and enduring the absolute loss of freedom really means. It isn't just those who Pinochet murdered, but the lives he stole from the living that must be accounted for too.

Sadly, Chile was not the only country in South America to be singled out for the U.S. government's attentions. Guatemala, Costa Rica, Ecuador, Brazil, Peru, the Dominican Republic, Bolivia, Nicaragua, Honduras, Panama, El Salvador, Peru, Mexico, and Colombia—they've all been the playground for covert—and overt—operations by the CIA.[70] Hundreds of thousands of Latin Americans have been killed, tortured, or have simply disappeared under the despotic regimes and tin-pot dictators, drug runners, and arms dealers that were propped up in their countries. (Many of them learned their craft in the infamous U.S. government–funded School of Americas in Fort Benning, Georgia, which has produced sixty thousand graduates.[71]) If this were not humiliation enough, the people of South America have had to bear the cross of being branded as a people who are incapable of democracy—as if coups and massacres are somehow encrypted in their genes.

This list does not of course include countries in Africa or Asia that suffered U.S. military interventions—Somalia, Vietnam, Korea, Indonesia, Laos, and Cambodia.[72] For how many Septembers for decades together have millions of Asian people been bombed, burned, and slaughtered? How many Septembers have gone by since August 1945, when hundreds of thousands of ordinary Japanese people were obliterated by the nuclear strikes in Hiroshima and Nagasaki? For how many Septembers have the thousands who had the misfortune of surviving those strikes endured the living hell that was visited on them, their unborn children, their children's children, on the earth, the sky, the wind, the water, and all the creatures that swim and walk and crawl and fly? Not far from here, in Albuquerque, is the National Atomic Museum, where Fat Man and Little Boy (the affectionate nicknames for the bombs that were dropped on Hiroshima and Nagasaki) were available as souvenir earrings. Funky young people wore them. A massacre dangling in each ear. But I am straying from my theme. It's September that we're talking about, not August.

September 11th has a tragic resonance in the Middle East too. On the 11th of September 1922, ignoring Arab outrage, the British government proclaimed a mandate in Palestine, a follow-up to the 1917 Balfour Declaration, which imperial Britain issued, with its army massed outside the gates of the city of Gaza.[73] The Balfour Declaration promised European Zionists "a national home for Jewish people."[74] (At the time, the empire on which the sun never set was free to snatch and bequeath national homes like the school bully distributes marbles.) Two years after the declaration, Lord Arthur James Balfour, the British foreign secretary said,

> [I]n Palestine we do not propose even to go through the form of consulting the wishes of the present inhabitants of the country.... Zionism, be it right or wrong, good or bad, is rooted in age-long tradition, in present needs, in future hopes, of far profounder import than the desires and prejudices of the 700,000 Arabs who now inhabit that ancient land.[75]

How carelessly imperial power decreed whose needs were profound and whose were not. How carelessly it vivisected ancient civilizations. Palestine and Kashmir are imperial Britain's festering, blood-drenched gifts to the modern world. Both are fault lines in the raging international conflicts of today.

In 1937 Winston Churchill said of the Palestinians:

> I do not agree that the dog in a manger has the final right to the manger, even though he may have lain there for a very long time. I do not admit that right. I do not admit, for instance, that a great wrong has been done to the Red Indians of America, or the black people of Australia. I do not admit that a wrong has been done to these people by the fact that a stronger race, a higher grade race, a more worldly-wise race, to put it that way, has come in and taken their place.[76]

That set the trend for the Israeli state's attitude toward Palestinians. In 1969, Israeli Prime Minister Golda Meir said, "Palestinians do not exist." Her successor, Prime Minister Levi Eshkol said, "Where are Palestinians? When I came here [to Palestine] there were 250,000 non-Jews, mainly Arabs and Bedouins. It was desert, more than underdeveloped. Nothing." Prime Minister Menachem Begin called Palestinians "two-legged beasts." Prime Minister Yitzhak Shamir called them "'grasshoppers' who could be crushed."[77] This is the language of heads of state, not the words of ordinary people. In 1947, the UN formally partitioned Palestine and allotted fifty-five percent of Palestine's land to the Zionists. Within a year they had captured more than seventy-six percent.[78] On the 14th of May 1948 the State of Israel was declared. Minutes after the declaration, the United States recognized Israel. The West Bank was annexed by Jordan. The Gaza strip came under the military control of Egypt.[79] Formally, Palestine ceased to exist except in the minds and hearts of the hundreds of thousands of Palestinian people who became refugees.

In the summer of 1967, Israel occupied the West Bank and the Gaza Strip. Settlers were offered state subsidies and development aid to move into the occupied territories. Almost every day more Palestinian families are forced off their lands and driven into refugee camps. Palestinians who continue to live in Israel do not have the same rights as Israelis and live as second-class citizens in their former homeland.[80]

Arundhati Roy

Over the decades there have been uprisings, wars, *inti-fadas*. Thousands have lost their lives.[81] Accords and treaties have been signed. Cease-fires declared and violated. But the bloodshed doesn't end. Palestine still remains illegally occupied. Its people live in inhuman conditions, in virtual Bantustans, where they are subjected to collective punishments and twenty-four hour curfews, where they are humiliated and brutalized on a daily basis. They never know when their homes will be demolished, when their children will be shot, when their precious trees will be cut, when their roads will be closed, when they will be allowed to walk down to the market to buy food and medicine. And when they will not. They live with no semblance of dignity. With not much hope in sight. They have no control over their lands, their security, their movement, their communication, their water supply. So when accords are signed and words like "autonomy" and even "statehood" are bandied about, it's always worth asking: What sort of autonomy? What sort of state? What sort of rights will its citizens have?

Young Palestinians who cannot contain their anger turn themselves into human bombs and haunt Israel's streets and public places, blowing themselves up, killing ordinary people, injecting terror into daily life, and eventually hardening both societies' suspicion and mutual hatred of each other. Each bombing invites merciless reprisals and even more hardship on Palestinian people. But then suicide bombing is an act of individual despair, not a revolutionary tactic. Although Palestinian attacks strike terror into Israeli civilians, they provide the perfect cover for the Israeli government's daily incursions into Palestinian territory, the perfect excuse for old-fashioned, nineteenth-century colonialism, dressed up as a new-fashioned, twenty-first century war.

Israel's staunchest political and military ally is and always has been the U.S. government. The U.S. government has blocked, along with Israel, almost every UN resolution that sought a peaceful, equitable solution to the conflict.[82] It has supported almost every war that Israel has fought. When Israel attacks Palestine, it is American missiles that smash through Palestinian homes. And every year Israel receives several billion dollars from the United States.[83]

What lessons should we draw from this tragic conflict? Is it really impossible for Jewish people who suffered so cruelly themselves—more cruelly perhaps than any other people in history—to understand the vulnerability and the yearning of those whom they have displaced? Does extreme suffering always kindle cruelty? What hope does this leave the human race with? What will happen to the Palestinian people in the event of a victory? When a nation without a state eventually proclaims a state, what kind of state will it be? What horrors will be perpetrated under its flag? Is it a separate state that we should be fighting for, or the rights to a life of liberty and dignity for everyone regardless of their ethnicity or religion?

Palestine was once a secular bulwark in the Middle East. But now the weak, undemocratic, by all accounts corrupt, but avowedly nonsectarian Palestinian Liberation Organization (PLO) is losing ground to Hamas, which espouses an overtly sectarian ideology and fights in the name of Islam. To quote from its manifesto: "We will be its soldiers and the firewood of its fire, which will burn the enemies."[84]

The world is called upon to condemn suicide bombers. But can we ignore the long road they have journeyed on before they arrived at this destination? September 11th, 1922, to September 11th, 2002—eighty years is a long, long time to have been waging war. Is there some advice the world can give the people of Palestine? Some scrap of hope we can hold out? Should they just settle for the crumbs that are thrown their way and behave like the grasshoppers or two-legged beasts they've been described as? Should they just take Golda Meir's suggestion and make a real effort to not exist?

In another part of the Middle East, September 11th strikes a more recent chord. It was on the 11th of September 1990 that George W. Bush Sr., then President of the United States, made a speech to a joint session of Congress announcing his government's decision to go to war against Iraq.[85]

The U.S. government says that Saddam Hussein is a war criminal, a cruel military despot who has committed genocide against his own people. That's a fairly accurate description of the man. In 1988 he razed hundreds of villages in northern Iraq and used chemical weapons and machine-guns to kill thousands of Kurdish people. Today we know that that same year the U.S. government provided him with five hundred million dollars in subsidies to buy American agricultural products. The next year, after he had successfully completed his genocidal campaign, the U.S. government doubled its subsidy to one billion dollars.[86] It also provided him with high quality germ seed for anthrax, as well as helicopters and dual-use material that could be used to manufacture chemical and biological weapons.[87]

So it turns out that while Saddam Hussein was carrying out his worst atrocities, the U.S. and the U.K. governments were his close allies. Even today, the government of Turkey, which has one of the most appalling human rights records in the world, is one of the U.S. government's closest allies. The fact that the Turkish government has oppressed and murdered Kurdish people for years has not prevented the U.S. government from plying Turkey with weapons and development aid.[88] Clearly it was not concern for the Kurdish people that provoked President Bush's speech to Congress.

What changed? In August 1990, Saddam Hussein invaded Kuwait. His sin was not so much that he had committed an act of war, but that he acted independently, without orders from his masters. This display of independence was enough to upset the power equation in the Gulf. So it was decided that Saddam Hussein be exterminated, like a pet that has outlived its owner's affection.

War Talk

The first Allied attack on Iraq took place in January 1991. The world watched the prime-time war as it was played out on TV. (In India those days, you had to go to a five-star hotel lobby to watch CNN.) Tens of thousands of people were killed in a month of devastating bombing.[89] What many do not know is that the war did not end then. The initial fury simmered down into the longest sustained air attack on a country since the Vietnam War. Over the last decade, American and British forces have fired thousands of missiles and bombs on Iraq. Iraq's fields and farmlands have been shelled with three hundred tons of depleted uranium.[90] In their bombing sorties, the Allies targeted and destroyed water treatment plants, aware of the fact that they could not be repaired without foreign assistance.[91] In southern Iraq, there has been a fourfold increase in cancer among children. In the decade of economic sanctions that followed the war, Iraqi civilians have been denied food, medicine, hospital equipment, ambulances, clean water—the basic essentials.[92]

About half a million Iraqi children have died as a result of the sanctions. Of them, Madeleine Albright, then U.S. Ambassador to the United Nations, famously said, "I think this is a very hard choice, but the price—we think the price is worth it." [93] "Moral equivalence" was the term that was used to denounce those who criticized the war on Afghanistan. Madeleine Albright cannot be accused of moral equivalence. What she said was just straightforward algebra.

A decade of bombing has not managed to dislodge Saddam Hussein, the "Beast of Baghdad." Now, almost twelve years on, President George Bush Jr. has ratcheted up the rhetoric once again. He's proposing an all-out war whose goal is nothing short of a "regime change." The *New York Times* says that the Bush administration is "following a meticulously planned strategy to persuade the public, the Congress and the allies of the need to confront the threat of Saddam Hussein." Andrew Card, the White House Chief of Staff, described how the administration was stepping up its war plans for the fall: "From a marketing point of view," he said, "you don't introduce new products in August." [94] This time the catchphrase for Washington's "new product" is not the plight of Kuwaiti people but the assertion that Iraq has weapons of mass destruction. Forget "the feckless moralising of 'peace' lobbies," wrote Richard Perle, chairman of the Defense Policy Board, the United States will "act alone if necessary" and use a "pre-emptive strike" if it determines it's in U.S. interests.[95]

Weapons inspectors have conflicting reports about the status of Iraq's "weapons of mass destruction," and many have said clearly that its arsenal has been dismantled and that it does not have the capacity to build one.[96] However, there is no confusion over the extent and range of America's arsenal of nuclear and chemical weapons. Would the U.S. government welcome weapons inspectors? Would the U.K.? Or Israel?

What if Iraq *does* have a nuclear weapon, does that justify a preemptive U.S. strike? The United States has the largest arsenal of nuclear weapons in the world. It's the only country in the world to have actually used them on civilian populations. If the United States is justified in launching a preemptive attack on Iraq, why then any nuclear power is justified in carrying out a preemptive attack on any other. India could attack Pakistan, or the other way around. If the U.S. government develops a distaste for the Indian Prime Minister, can it just "take him out" with a preemptive strike?

Recently the United States played an important part in forcing India and Pakistan back from the brink of war.

Is it so hard for it to take its own advice? Who is guilty of feckless moralizing? Of preaching peace while it wages war? The United States, which George Bush calls "a peaceful nation," has been at war with one country or another every year for the last fifty years.[97]

Wars are never fought for altruistic reasons. They're usually fought for hegemony, for business. And then of course, there's the business of war. Protecting its control of the world's oil is fundamental to U.S. foreign policy. The U.S. government's recent military interventions in the Balkans and Central Asia have to do with oil. Hamid Karzai, the puppet president of Afghanistan installed by the United States, is said to be a former employee of Unocal, the American-based oil company.[98] The U.S. government's paranoid patrolling of the Middle East is because it has two-thirds of the world's oil reserves.[99] Oil keeps America's engines purring sweetly. Oil keeps the free market rolling. Whoever controls the world's oil controls the world's markets.

And how do you control the oil? Nobody puts it more elegantly than the *New York Times'* columnist Thomas Friedman. In an article called "Craziness Pays," he says "the U.S. has to make clear to Iraq and U.S. allies that…America will use force, without negotiation, hesitation, or UN approval."[100] His advice was well taken. In the wars against Iraq and Afghanistan, as well as in the almost daily humiliation the U.S. government heaps on the UN. In his book on globalization, *The Lexus and the Olive Tree,* Friedman says, "The hidden hand of the market will never work without a hidden fist. McDonald's cannot flourish without McDonnell Douglas…. And the hidden fist that keeps the world safe for Silicon Valley's technologies to flourish is called the U.S. Army, Air Force, Navy, and Marine Corps."[101]

Perhaps this was written in a moment of vulnerability, but it's certainly the most succinct, accurate description of the project of corporate globalization that I have read.

After September 11th, 2001, and the War Against Terror, the hidden hand and fist have had their cover blown, and we have a clear view now of America's other weapon—the free market—bearing down on the developing world, with a clenched unsmiling smile. The Task That Does Not End is America's perfect war, the perfect vehicle for the endless expansion of American imperialism. In Urdu, the word for profit is *fayda. Al Qaida* means The Word, The Word of God, The Law. So, in India some of us call the War Against Terror, *Al Qaida* versus *Al Fayda*—The Word versus The Profit (no pun intended).

For the moment it looks as though *Al Fayda* will carry the day. But then you never know...

In the last ten years of unbridled corporate globalization, the world's total income has increased by an average of 2.5 percent a year. And yet the numbers of the poor in the world has increased by one hundred million. Of the top hundred biggest economies, fifty-one are corporations, not countries. The top one percent of the world has the same combined income as the bottom fifty-seven percent and the disparity is growing.[102] Now, under the spreading canopy of the War Against Terror, this process is being hustled along. The men in suits are in an unseemly hurry. While bombs rain down on us, and cruise missiles skid across the skies, while nuclear weapons are stockpiled to make the world a safer place, contracts are being signed, patents are being registered, oil pipelines are being laid, natural resources are being plundered, water is being privatized, and democracies are being undermined.

In a country like India, the "structural adjustment" end of the corporate globalization project is ripping through people's lives. "Development" projects, massive privatization, and labor "reforms" are pushing people off their lands and out of their jobs, resulting in a kind of barbaric dispossession that has few parallels in history. Across the world as the free market brazenly protects Western markets and forces developing countries to lift their trade barriers, the poor are getting poorer and the rich richer. Civil unrest has begun to erupt in the global village. In countries like Argentina, Brazil, Mexico, Bolivia, and India, the resistance movements against corporate globalization are growing. To contain them, governments are tightening their control. Protesters are being labeled "terrorists" and then being dealt with as such. But civil unrest does not only mean marches and demonstrations and protests against globalization. Unfortunately, it also means a desperate downward spiral into crime and chaos and all kinds of despair and disillusionment which, as we know from history (and from what we see unspooling before our eyes), gradually becomes a fertile breeding ground for terrible things—cultural nationalism, religious bigotry, fascism, and of course terrorism.

All these march arm in arm with corporate globalization.

Arundhati Roy

There is a notion gaining credence that the free market breaks down national barriers, and that corporate globalization's ultimate destination is a hippie paradise where the heart is the only passport and we all live together happily inside a John Lennon song (*Imagine there's no country…*). This is a canard.

What the free market undermines is not national sovereignty, but *democracy*. As the disparity between the rich and poor grows, the hidden fist has its work cut out for it. Multinational corporations on the prowl for sweetheart deals that yield enormous profits cannot push through those deals and administer those projects in developing countries without the active connivance of state machinery—the police, the courts, sometimes even the army. Today corporate globalization needs an international confederation of loyal, corrupt, authoritarian governments in poorer countries to push through unpopular reforms and quell the mutinies. It needs a press that pretends to be free. It needs courts that pretend to dispense justice. It needs nuclear bombs, standing armies, sterner immigration laws, and watchful coastal patrols to make sure that it's only money, goods, patents, and services that are globalized—not the free movement of people, not a respect for hu-

man rights, not international treaties on racial discrimination, or chemical and nuclear weapons, or greenhouse gas
emissions, climate change, or, god forbid, justice.[103] It's as
though even a *gesture* toward international accountability
would wreck the whole enterprise.

Close to one year after the War Against Terror was
officially flagged off in the ruins of Afghanistan, freedoms
are being curtailed in country after country in the name of
protecting freedom, civil liberties are being suspended in
the name of protecting democracy.[104] All kinds of dissent
is being defined as "terrorism." All kinds of laws are being
passed to deal with it. Osama bin Laden seems to have
vanished into thin air. Mullah Omar is said to have made
his escape on a motorbike.[105] (They could have sent
Tin-Tin after him.) The Taliban may have disappeared
but their spirit, and their system of summary justice, is
surfacing in the unlikeliest of places. In India, in Pakistan,
in Nigeria, in America, in all the Central Asian republics
run by all manner of despots, and of course in Afghanistan under the U.S.-backed Northern Alliance.[106]

Meanwhile down at the mall there's a mid-season
sale. Everything's discounted—oceans, rivers, oil, gene
pools, fig wasps, flowers, childhoods, aluminum facto-

ries, phone companies, wisdom, wilderness, civil rights, ecosystems, air—all 4.6 billion years of evolution. It's packed, sealed, tagged, valued, and available off the rack (no returns). As for justice—I'm told it's on offer too. You can get the best that money can buy.

Donald Rumsfeld said that his mission in the War Against Terror was to persuade the world that Americans must be allowed to continue their way of life.[107] When the maddened king stamps his foot, slaves tremble in their quarters. So, standing here today, it's hard for me to say this, but The American Way of Life is simply not sustainable. Because it doesn't acknowledge that there is a world beyond America.

Fortunately power has a shelf life. When the time comes, maybe this mighty empire will, like others before it, overreach itself and implode from within. It looks as though structural cracks have already appeared. As the War Against Terror casts its net wider and wider, America's corporate heart is hemorrhaging. For all the endless empty chatter about democracy, today the world is run by three of the most secretive institutions in the world: the International Monetary Fund, the World Bank, and the World Trade Organization, all three of which, in turn, are dominated by the United States. Their decisions are made in secret. The people who head them are appointed behind closed doors. Nobody really knows anything about them, their politics, their beliefs, their intentions. Nobody elected them. Nobody said they could make decisions on our behalf. A world run by a handful of greedy bankers and CEOs who nobody elected can't possibly last.

Soviet-style communism failed, not because it was intrinsically evil, but because it was flawed. It allowed too few people to usurp too much power. Twenty-first century market capitalism, American-style, will fail for the same reasons. Both are edifices constructed by human intelligence, undone by human nature.

The time has come, the Walrus said. Perhaps things will get worse and then better. Perhaps there's a small god up in heaven readying herself for us. Another world is not only possible, she's on her way. Maybe many of us won't be here to greet her, but on a quiet day, if I listen very carefully, I can hear her breathing.

THE LONELINESS OF
NOAM CHOMSKY

"I will never apologize for the United States of America—I don't care what the facts are."

—President George Bush Sr.[108]

Sitting in my home in New Delhi, watching an American TV news channel promote itself ("We report. You decide"), I imagine Noam Chomsky's amused, chipped-tooth smile.

Everybody knows that authoritarian regimes, regardless of their ideology, use the mass media for propaganda. But what about democratically elected regimes in the "free world"?

Written as an introduction for the new edition of Noam Chomsky's *For Reasons of State* (New York: New Press, 2003).

Arundhati Roy

Today, thanks to Noam Chomsky and his fellow media analysts, it is almost axiomatic for thousands, possibly millions, of us that public opinion in "free market" democracies is manufactured just like any other mass market product—soap, switches, or sliced bread.[109] We know that while, legally and constitutionally, speech may be free, the space in which that freedom can be exercised has been snatched from us and auctioned to the highest bidders. Neoliberal capitalism isn't just about the accumulation of capital (for some). It's also about the accumulation of power (for some), the accumulation of freedom (for some). Conversely, for the rest of the world, the people who are excluded from neoliberalism's governing body, it's about the *erosion* of capital, the *erosion* of power, the *erosion* of freedom. In the "free" market, free speech has become a commodity like everything else—justice, human rights, drinking water, clean air. It's available only to those who can afford it. And naturally, those who can afford it use free speech to manufacture the kind of product, confect the kind of public opinion, that best suits their purpose. (News they can use.) Exactly how they do this has been the subject of much of Noam Chomsky's political writing.

War Talk

Prime Minister Silvio Berlusconi, for instance, has a controlling interest in major Italian newspapers, magazines, television channels, and publishing houses. "[T]he prime minister in effect controls about 90 percent of Italian TV viewership," reports the *Financial Times*.[110] What price free speech? Free speech for *whom?* Admittedly, Berlusconi is an extreme example. In other democracies—the United States in particular—media barons, powerful corporate lobbies, and government officials are imbricated in a more elaborate but less obvious manner. (George Bush Jr.'s connections to the oil lobby, to the arms industry, and to Enron, and Enron's infiltration of U.S. government institutions and the mass media—all this is public knowledge now.)

After the September 11, 2001, terrorist strikes in New York and Washington, the mainstream media's blatant performance as the U.S. government's mouthpiece, its display of vengeful patriotism, its willingness to publish Pentagon press handouts as news, and its explicit censorship of dissenting opinion became the butt of some pretty black humor in the rest of the world.

Then the New York Stock Exchange crashed, bankrupt airline companies appealed to the government for financial bailouts, and there was talk of circumventing patent laws in order to manufacture generic drugs to fight the anthrax scare (*much* more important and urgent of course than the production of generics to fight AIDS in Africa).[111] Suddenly, it began to seem as though the twin myths of Free Speech and the Free Market might come crashing down alongside the Twin Towers of the World Trade Center.

But of course that never happened. The myths live on.

There is however, a brighter side to the amount of energy and money that the establishment pours into the business of "managing" public opinion. It suggests a very real *fear* of public opinion. It suggests a persistent and valid worry that if people were to discover (and fully comprehend) the real nature of the things that are done in their name, they might *act* upon that knowledge. Powerful people know that ordinary people are not always reflexively ruthless and selfish. (When ordinary people weigh costs and benefits, something like an uneasy conscience could easily tip the scales.) For this reason, they must be guarded against reality, reared in a controlled climate, in an altered reality, like broiler chickens or pigs in a pen.

Those of us who have managed to escape this fate and are scratching about in the backyard, no longer believe everything we read in the papers and watch on TV. We put our ears to the ground and look for other ways of making sense of the world. We search for the untold story, the mentioned-in-passing military coup, the unreported genocide, the civil war in an African country written up in a one-column-inch story next to a full-page advertisement for lace underwear.

We don't always remember, and many don't even know, that this way of thinking, this easy acuity, this instinctive mistrust of the mass media, would at best be a political hunch and at worst a loose accusation, if it were not for the relentless and unswerving media analysis of one of the world's greatest minds. And this is only *one* of the ways in which Noam Chomsky has radically altered our understanding of the society in which we live. Or should I say, our understanding of the elaborate rules of the lunatic asylum in which we are all voluntary inmates?

Speaking about the September 11 attacks in New York and Washington, President George W. Bush called the enemies of the United States "enemies of freedom." "Americans are asking why do they hate us?" he said. "They hate our freedoms, our freedom of religion, our freedom of speech, our freedom to vote and assemble and disagree with each other." [112]

If people in the United States want a real answer to that question (as opposed to the ones in the *Idiot's Guide to Anti-Americanism,* that is: "Because they're jealous of us," "Because they hate freedom," "Because they're losers," "Because we're good and they're evil"), I'd say, read Chomsky. Read Chomsky on U.S. military interventions in Indochina, Latin America, Iraq, Bosnia, the former Yugoslavia, Afghanistan, and the Middle East. If ordinary people in the United States read Chomsky, perhaps their questions would be framed a little differently. Perhaps it would be: "Why don't they hate us more than they do?" or "Isn't it surprising that September 11 didn't happen earlier?"

Unfortunately, in these nationalistic times, words like "us" and "them" are used loosely. The line between citizens and the state is being deliberately and successfully blurred, not just by governments, but also by terrorists. The underlying logic of terrorist attacks, as well as "retaliatory" wars against governments that "support terrorism," is the same: both punish citizens for the actions of their governments.

War Talk

(A brief digression: I realize that for Noam Chomsky, a U.S. citizen, to criticize his own government is better manners than for someone like myself, an Indian citizen, to criticize the U.S. government. I'm no patriot, and am fully aware that venality, brutality, and hypocrisy are imprinted on the leaden soul of every state. But when a country ceases to be merely a country and becomes an empire, then the scale of operations changes dramatically. So may I clarify that I speak as a subject of the U.S. empire? I speak as a slave who presumes to criticize her king.)

If I were asked to choose *one* of Noam Chomsky's major contributions to the world, it would be the fact that he has unmasked the ugly, manipulative, ruthless universe that exists behind that beautiful, sunny word "freedom." He has done this rationally and empirically. The mass of evidence he has marshaled to construct his case is formidable. Terrifying, actually. The starting premise of Chomsky's method is not ideological, but it *is* intensely political. He embarks on his course of inquiry with an anarchist's instinctive mistrust of power. He takes us on a tour through the bog of the U.S. establishment, and leads us through the dizzying maze of corridors that connects the government, big business, and the business of managing public opinion.

Chomsky shows us how phrases like "free speech," the "free market," and the "free world" have little, if anything, to do with freedom. He shows us that, among the myriad freedoms claimed by the U.S. government are the freedom to murder, annihilate, and dominate other people. The freedom to finance and sponsor despots and dictators across the world. The freedom to train, arm, and shelter terrorists. The freedom to topple democratically elected governments. The freedom to amass and use weapons of mass destruction—chemical, biological, and nuclear. The freedom to go to war against any country whose government it disagrees with. And, most terrible of all, the freedom to commit these crimes against humanity in the name of "justice," in the name of "righteousness," in the name of "freedom."

Attorney General John Ashcroft has declared that U.S. freedoms are "not the grant of any government or document, but…our endowment from God."[113] So, basically, we're confronted with a country armed with a mandate from heaven. Perhaps this explains why the U.S. government refuses to judge itself by the same moral standards by which it judges others. (Any attempt to do this is shouted down as "moral equivalence.") Its technique is to position itself as the well-intentioned giant whose good deeds are confounded in strange countries by their scheming natives, whose markets it's trying to free, whose societies it's trying to modernize, whose women it's trying to liberate, whose souls it's trying to save.

Perhaps this belief in its own divinity also explains why the U.S. government has conferred upon itself the right and freedom to murder and exterminate people "for their own good."

When he announced the U.S. air strikes against Afghanistan, President Bush Jr. said, "We're a peaceful nation."[114] He went on to say, "This is the calling of the United States of America, the most free nation in the world, a nation built on fundamental values, that rejects hate, rejects violence, rejects murderers, rejects evil. And we will not tire."[115]

The U.S. empire rests on a grisly foundation: the massacre of millions of indigenous people, the stealing of their lands, and following this, the kidnapping and enslavement of millions of black people from Africa to work that land. Thousands died on the seas while they were being shipped like caged cattle between continents.[116] "Stolen from Africa, brought to America"—Bob Marley's "Buffalo Soldier" contains a whole universe of unspeakable sadness.[117] It tells of the loss of dignity, the loss of wilderness, the loss of freedom, the shattered pride of a people. Genocide and slavery provide the social and economic underpinning of the nation whose fundamental values reject hate, murderers, and evil.

Here is Chomsky, writing in the essay "The Manufacture of Consent," on the founding of the United States of America:

> During the Thanksgiving holiday a few weeks ago, I took a walk with some friends and family in a national park. We came across a gravestone, which had on it the following inscription: "Here lies an Indian woman, a Wampanoag, whose family and tribe gave of themselves and their land that this great nation might be born and grow."
>
> Of course, it is not quite accurate to say that the indigenous population gave of themselves and their land for that noble purpose. Rather, they were slaughtered, decimated, and dispersed in the course of one of the greatest exercises in genocide in human history…which we celebrate each October when we honor Columbus—a notable mass murderer himself—on Columbus Day.

War Talk

Hundreds of American citizens, well-meaning and decent people, troop by that gravestone regularly and read it, apparently without reaction; except, perhaps, a feeling of satisfaction that at last we are giving some due recognition to the sacrifices of the native peoples.... They might react differently if they were to visit Auschwitz or Dachau and find a gravestone reading: "Here lies a woman, a Jew, whose family and people gave of themselves and their possessions that this great nation might grow and prosper."[118]

How has the United States survived its terrible past and emerged smelling so sweet? Not by owning up to it, not by making reparations, not by apologizing to black Americans or native Americans, and certainly not by changing its ways (it *exports* its cruelties now). Like most other countries, the United States has rewritten its history. But what sets the United States apart from other countries, and puts it way ahead in the race, is that it has enlisted the services of the most powerful, most successful publicity firm in the world: Hollywood.

In the best-selling version of popular myth as history, U.S. "goodness" peaked during World War II (*aka* America's War Against Fascism). Lost in the din of trumpet sound and angel song is the fact that when fascism was in full stride in Europe, the U.S. government actually looked away. When Hitler was carrying out his genocidal pogrom against Jews, U.S. officials refused entry to Jewish refugees fleeing Germany. The United States entered the war only *after* the Japanese bombed Pearl Harbor. Drowned out by the noisy hosannas is its most barbaric act, in fact the single most savage act the world has ever witnessed: the dropping of the atomic bomb on civilian populations in Hiroshima and Nagasaki. The war was nearly over. The hundreds of thousands of Japanese people who were killed, the countless others who were crippled by cancers for generations to come, were not a threat to world peace. They were *civilians*. Just as the victims of the World Trade Center and Pentagon bombings were civilians. Just as the hundreds of thousands of people who died in Iraq because of the U.S.-led sanctions were civilians. The bombing of Hiroshima and Nagasaki was a cold, calculated experiment carried out to demonstrate America's power. At the time, President Truman described it as "the greatest thing in history."[119]

The Second World War, we're told, was a "war for peace." The atomic bomb was a "weapon of peace."

War Talk

We're invited to believe that nuclear deterrence prevented World War III. (That was before President George Bush Jr. came up with the "pre-emptive strike doctrine."[120]) *Was* there an outbreak of peace after the Second World War? Certainly there was (relative) peace in Europe and America—but does that count as world peace? Not unless savage, proxy wars fought in lands where the colored races live (chinks, niggers, dinks, wogs, gooks) don't count as wars at all.

Since the Second World War, the United States has been at war with or has attacked, among other countries, Korea, Guatemala, Cuba, Laos, Vietnam, Cambodia, Grenada, Libya, El Salvador, Nicaragua, Panama, Iraq, Somalia, Sudan, Yugoslavia, and Afghanistan. This list should also include the U.S. government's covert operations in Africa, Asia, and Latin America, the coups it has engineered, and the dictators it has armed and supported. It should include Israel's U.S.-backed war on Lebanon, in which thousands were killed. It should include the key role America has played in the conflict in the Middle East, in which thousands have died fighting Israel's illegal occupation of Palestinian territory. It should include America's role in the civil war in Afghanistan in the 1980s, in which more than one million people were killed.[121] It should include the embargos and sanctions that have led directly and indirectly to the death of hundreds of thousands of people, most visibly in Iraq.[122] Put it all together, and it sounds very much as though there has been a World War III, and that the U.S. government was (or is) one of its chief protagonists.

Most of the essays in Chomsky's *For Reasons of State* are about U.S. aggression in South Vietnam, North Vietnam, Laos, and Cambodia. It was a war that lasted more than twelve years. Fifty-eight thousand Americans and approximately two million Vietnamese, Cambodians, and Laotians lost their lives.[123] The U.S. deployed half a million ground troops, dropped more than six million tons of bombs.[124] And yet, though you wouldn't believe it if you watched most Hollywood movies, America lost the war.

The war began in South Vietnam and then spread to North Vietnam, Laos, and Cambodia. After putting in place a client regime in Saigon, the U.S. government invited itself in to fight a communist insurgency—Vietcong guerillas who had infiltrated rural regions of South Vietnam where villagers were sheltering them. This was exactly the model that Russia replicated when, in 1979, it invited itself into Afghanistan. Nobody in the "free world" is in any doubt about the fact that Russia invaded Afghanistan. After *glasnost,* even a Soviet foreign minister called the Soviet invasion of Afghanistan "illegal and immoral."[125] But there has been no such introspection in the United States. In 1984, in a stunning revelation, Chomsky wrote:

> For the past twenty-two years, I have been searching to find some reference in mainstream journalism or scholarship to an American invasion of South Vietnam in 1962 (or ever), or an American attack against South Vietnam, or American aggression in Indochina—without success. There is no such event in history. Rather, there is an American *defense* of South Vietnam against terrorists supported from the outside (namely from Vietnam).[126]

There is no such event in history!

In 1962, the U.S. Air Force began to bomb rural South Vietnam, where eighty percent of the population lived. The bombing lasted for more than a decade. Thousands of people were killed. The idea was to bomb on a scale colossal enough to induce panic migration from villages into cities, where people could be held in refugee camps. Samuel Huntington referred to this as a process of "urbanization."[127] (I learned about urbanization when I was in architecture school in India. Somehow I don't remember aerial bombing being part of the syllabus.) Huntington—famous today for his essay "The Clash of Civilizations?"—was at the time Chairman of the Council on Vietnamese Studies of the Southeast Asia Development Advisory Group. Chomsky quotes him describing the Vietcong as "a powerful force which cannot be dislodged from its constituency so long as the constituency continues to exist."[128] Huntington went on to advise "direct application of mechanical and conventional power"—in other words, to crush a people's war, eliminate the people.[129] (Or, perhaps, to update the thesis—in order to prevent a clash of civilizations, annihilate a civilization.)

Here's one observer from the time on the limitations of America's mechanical power: "The problem is that American machines are not equal to the task of killing communist soldiers except as part of a scorched-earth policy that destroys everything else as well."[130] That problem has been solved now. Not with less destructive bombs, but with more imaginative language. There's a more elegant way of saying "that destroys everything else as well." The phrase is "collateral damage."

And here's a firsthand account of what America's "machines" (Huntington called them "modernizing instruments" and staff officers in the Pentagon called them "bomb-o-grams") can do.[131] This is T.D. Allman flying over the Plain of Jars in Laos.

> Even if the war in Laos ended tomorrow, the restoration of its ecological balance might take several years. The reconstruction of the Plain's totally destroyed towns and villages might take just as long. Even if this was done, the Plain might long prove perilous to human habitation because of the hundreds of thousands of unexploded bombs, mines and booby traps.
>
> A recent flight around the Plain of Jars revealed what less than three years of intensive American bombing can do to a rural area, even after its civilian population has been evacuated. In large areas, the primary tropical colour—bright green—has been replaced by an abstract pattern of black, and bright metallic colours. Much of the remaining foliage is stunted, dulled by defoliants.

Today, black is the dominant colour of the northern and eastern reaches of the Plain. Napalm is dropped regularly to burn off the grass and undergrowth that covers the Plains and fills its many narrow ravines. The fires seem to burn constantly, creating rectangles of black. During the flight, plumes of smoke could be seen rising from freshly bombed areas.

The main routes, coming into the Plain from communist-held territory, are bombed mercilessly, apparently on a non-stop basis. There, and along the rim of the Plain, the dominant colour is yellow. All vegetation has been destroyed. The craters are countless.... [T]he area has been bombed so repeatedly that the land resembles the pocked, churned desert in storm-hit areas of the North African desert.

Further to the southeast, Xieng Khouangville—once the most populous town in communist Laos—lies empty, destroyed. To the north of the Plain, the little resort of Khang Khay also has been destroyed.

Around the landing field at the base of King Kong, the main colours are yellow (from up-turned soil) and black (from napalm), relieved by patches of bright red and blue: parachutes used to drop supplies.

[T]he last local inhabitants were being carted into air transports. Abandoned vegetable gardens that would never be harvested grew near abandoned houses with plates still on the tables and calendars on the walls.[132]

(Never counted in the "costs" of war are the dead birds, the charred animals, the murdered fish, incinerated insects, poisoned water sources, destroyed vegetation. Rarely mentioned is the arrogance of the human race toward other living things with which it shares this planet. All these are forgotten in the fight for markets and ideologies. This arrogance will probably be the ultimate undoing of the human species.)

The centerpiece of *For Reasons of State* is an essay called "The Mentality of the Backroom Boys," in which Chomsky offers an extraordinarily supple, exhaustive analysis of the Pentagon Papers, which he says "provide documentary evidence of a conspiracy to use force in international affairs in violation of law."[133] Here, too, Chomsky makes note of the fact that while the bombing of North Vietnam is discussed at some length in the Pentagon Papers, the invasion of South Vietnam barely merits a mention.[134]

The Pentagon Papers are mesmerizing, not as documentation of the history of the U.S. war in Indochina, but as insight into the minds of the men who planned and executed it. It's fascinating to be privy to the ideas that were being tossed around, the suggestions that were made, the proposals that were put forward. In a section called "The Asian Mind—the American Mind," Chomsky examines the discussion of the mentality of the enemy that "stoically accept[s] the destruction of wealth and the loss of lives," whereas "We want life, happiness, wealth, power," and, for us, "death and suffering are irrational choices when alternatives exist."[135] So, we learn that the Asian poor, presumably because they cannot comprehend the meaning of happiness, wealth, and power, invite America to carry this "strategic logic to its conclusion, which is genocide." But, then "we" balk because "genocide is a terrible burden to bear."[136] (Eventually, of course, "we" went ahead and committed genocide any way, and then pretended that it never really happened.)

Of course, the Pentagon Papers contain some moderate proposals, as well.

Strikes at population targets (per se) are likely not only to create a counterproductive wave of revulsion abroad and at home, but greatly to increase the risk of enlarging the war with China and the Soviet Union. Destruction of locks and dams, however—if handled right—might...offer promise. It should be studied. Such destruction does not kill or drown people. By shallow-flooding the rice, it leads after time to widespread starvation (more than a million?) unless food is provided—which we could offer to do "at the conference table."[137]

Layer by layer, Chomsky strips down the process of decision-making by U.S. government officials, to reveal at its core the pitiless heart of the American war machine, completely insulated from the realities of war, blinded by ideology, and willing to annihilate millions of human beings, civilians, soldiers, women, children, villages, whole cities, whole ecosystems—with scientifically honed methods of brutality.

Here's an American pilot talking about the joys of napalm:

We sure are pleased with those backroom boys at Dow. The original product wasn't so hot—if the gooks were quick they could scrape it off. So the boys started adding polystyrene—now it sticks like shit to a blanket. But then if the gooks jumped under water it stopped burning, so they started adding Willie Peter [white phosphorous] so's to make it burn better. It'll even burn under water now. And just one drop is enough, it'll keep on burning right down to the bone so they die anyway from phosphorous poisoning.[138]

So the lucky gooks were annihilated for their own good. Better Dead than Red.

Thanks to the seductive charms of Hollywood and the irresistible appeal of America's mass media, all these years later, the world views the war as an *American* story. Indochina provided the lush, tropical backdrop against which the United States played out its fantasies of violence, tested its latest technology, furthered its ideology, examined its conscience, agonized over its moral dilemmas, and dealt with its guilt (or pretended to). The Vietnamese, the Cambodians, and Laotians were only script props. Nameless, faceless, slit-eyed humanoids. They were just the people who died. Gooks.

The only real lesson the U.S. government learned from its invasion of Indochina is how to go to war without committing American troops and risking American lives. So now we have wars waged with long-range cruise missiles, Black Hawks, "bunker busters." Wars in which the "Allies" lose more journalists than soldiers.

As a child growing up in the state of Kerala, in South India—where the first democratically elected Communist government in the world came to power in 1959, the year I was born—I worried terribly about being a gook. Kerala was only a few thousand miles west of Vietnam. We had jungles and rivers and rice-fields, and communists, too. I kept imagining my mother, my brother, and myself being blown out of the bushes by a grenade, or mowed down, like the gooks in the movies, by an American marine with muscled arms and chewing gum and a loud background score. In my dreams, I was the burning girl in the famous photograph taken on the road from Trang Bang.

As someone who grew up on the cusp of both American and Soviet propaganda (which more or less neutralized each other), when I first read Noam Chomsky, it occurred to me that his marshaling of evidence, the volume of it, the relentlessness of it, was a little—how shall I put it?—insane. Even a quarter of the evidence he had compiled would have been enough to convince me. I used to wonder why he needed to do so much *work*. But now I understand that the magnitude and intensity of Chomsky's work is a barometer of the magnitude, scope, and relentlessness of the propaganda machine that he's up against. He's like the wood-borer who lives inside the third rack of my bookshelf. Day and night, I hear his jaws crunching through the wood, grinding it to a fine dust. It's as though he disagrees with the literature and wants to destroy the very structure on which it rests. I call him Chompsky.

Being an American working in America, writing to convince Americans of his point of view must really be like having to tunnel through hard wood. Chomsky is one of a small band of individuals fighting a whole industry. And that makes him not only brilliant, but heroic.

Some years ago, in a poignant interview with James Peck, Chomsky spoke about his memory of the day Hiroshima was bombed. He was sixteen years old:

I remember that I literally couldn't talk to anybody. There was nobody. I just walked off by myself. I was at a summer camp at the time, and I walked off into the woods and stayed alone for a couple of hours when I heard about it. I could never talk to anyone about it and never understood anyone's reaction. I felt completely isolated.[139]

That isolation produced one of the greatest, most radical public thinkers of our time.

When the sun sets on the American empire, as it will, as it must, Noam Chomsky's work will survive. It will point a cool, incriminating finger at a merciless, Machiavellian empire as cruel, self-righteous, and hypocritical as the ones it has replaced. (The only difference is that it is armed with technology that can visit the kind of devastation on the world that history has never known and the human race cannot begin to imagine.)

As a could've been gook, and who knows, perhaps a potential gook, hardly a day goes by when I don't find myself thinking—for one reason or another—"Chomsky Zindabad."

CONFRONTING EMPIRE

I've been asked to speak about "How to confront Empire?" It's a huge question, and I have no easy answers.

When we speak of confronting Empire, we need to identify what Empire means. Does it mean the U.S. government (and its European satellites), the World Bank, the International Monetary Fund, the World Trade Organization (WTO), and multinational corporations? Or is it something more than that?

In many countries, Empire has sprouted other subsidiary heads, some dangerous byproducts—nationalism, religious bigotry, fascism and, of course, terrorism. All these march arm in arm with the project of corporate globalization.

First presented at the closing rally of the World Social Forum in Porto Alegre, Brazil, January 27, 2003.

Let me illustrate what I mean. India—the world's biggest democracy—is currently at the forefront of the corporate globalization project. Its "market" of one billion people is being pried open by the WTO. Corporatization and privatization are being welcomed by the government and the Indian elite.

It is not a coincidence that the Prime Minister, the Home Minister, the Disinvestment Minister—the men who signed the deal with Enron in India, the men who are selling the country's infrastructure to corporate multinationals, the men who want to privatize water, electricity, oil, coal, steel, health, education, and telecommunication—are all members or admirers of the Rashtriya Swayamsevak Sangh (RSS), a right wing, ultra-nationalist Hindu guild which has openly admired Hitler and his methods.

The dismantling of democracy is proceeding with the speed and efficiency of a Structural Adjustment Program. While the project of corporate globalization rips through people's lives in India, massive privatization and labor "reforms" are pushing people off their land and out of their jobs. Hundreds of impoverished farmers are committing suicide by consuming pesticide.[140]

Reports of starvation deaths are coming in from all over the country.[141]

While the elite journeys to its imaginary destination somewhere near the top of the world, the dispossessed are spiraling downwards into crime and chaos. This climate of frustration and national disillusionment is the perfect breeding ground, history tells us, for fascism.

The two arms of the Indian government have evolved the perfect pincer action. While one arm is busy selling India off in chunks, the other, to divert attention, is orchestrating a howling, baying chorus of Hindu nationalism and religious fascism. It is conducting nuclear tests, rewriting history books, burning churches, and demolishing mosques. Censorship, surveillance, the suspension of civil liberties and human rights, the questioning of who is an Indian citizen and who is not, particularly with regard to religious minorities, are all becoming common practice now.

Last March, in the state of Gujarat, two thousand Muslims were butchered in a state-sponsored pogrom. Muslim women were specially targeted. They were stripped, and gang-raped, before being burned alive. Arsonists burned and looted shops, homes, textiles mills, and mosques.[142]

More than a hundred and fifty thousand Muslims have been driven from their homes. The economic base of the Muslim community has been devastated.

While Gujarat burned, the Indian Prime Minister was on MTV promoting his new poems. In December 2002, the government that orchestrated the killing was voted back into office with a comfortable majority.[143] Nobody has been punished for the genocide. Narendra Modi, architect of the pogrom, proud member of the RSS, has embarked on his second term as the Chief Minister of Gujarat. If he were Saddam Hussein, of course each atrocity would have been on CNN. But since he's not—and since the Indian "market" is open to global investors—the massacre is not even an embarrassing inconvenience.

There are more than one hundred million Muslims in India. A time bomb is ticking in our ancient land.

All this to say that it is a myth that the free market breaks down national barriers. The free market does not threaten national sovereignty, it undermines democracy.

As the disparity between the rich and the poor grows, the fight to corner resources is intensifying. To push through their "sweetheart deals," to corporatize the crops we grow, the water we drink, the air we breathe, and the dreams we dream, corporate globalization needs an international confederation of loyal, corrupt, authoritarian governments in poorer countries to push through unpopular reforms and quell the mutinies.

Corporate globalization—or shall we call it by its name?—Imperialism—needs a press that pretends to be free. It needs courts that pretend to dispense justice.

Meanwhile, the countries of the North harden their borders and stockpile weapons of mass destruction. After all they have to make sure that it's only money, goods, patents, and services that are globalized. Not the free movement of people. Not a respect for human rights. Not international treaties on racial discrimination or chemical and nuclear weapons or greenhouse gas emissions or climate change or—god forbid—justice.

So this—*all* this—is Empire. This loyal confederation, this obscene accumulation of power, this greatly increased distance between those who make the decisions and those who have to suffer them.

Our fight, our goal, our vision of another world must be to eliminate that distance.

So how do we resist Empire?

The good news is that we're not doing too badly. There have been major victories. Here in Latin America you have had so many—in Bolivia, you have Cochabamba.[144] In Peru, there was the uprising in Arequipa.[145] In Venezuela, President Hugo Chavez is holding on, despite the U.S. government's best efforts.[146]

And the world's gaze is on the people of Argentina, who are trying to refashion a country from the ashes of the havoc wrought by the IMF.[147]

In India the movement against corporate globalization is gathering momentum and is poised to become the only real political force to counter religious fascism.

As for corporate globalization's glittering ambassadors —Enron, Bechtel, WorldCom, Arthur Andersen— where were they last year, and where are they now?

And of course here in Brazil we must ask: who was the president last year, and who is it now?

Still, many of us have dark moments of hopelessness and despair. We know that under the spreading canopy of the War Against Terrorism, the men in suits are hard at work.

While bombs rain down on us and cruise missiles skid across the skies, we know that contracts are being signed, patents are being registered, oil pipelines are being laid, natural resources are being plundered, water is being privatized, and George Bush is planning to go to war against Iraq.

If we look at this conflict as a straightforward eye-ball to eye-ball confrontation between Empire and those of us who are resisting it, it might seem that we are losing.

But there is another way of looking at it. We, all of us gathered here, have, each in our own way, laid siege to Empire.

We may not have stopped it in its tracks—yet—but we have stripped it down. We have made it drop its mask. We have forced it into the open. It now stands before us on the world's stage in all it's brutish, iniquitous nakedness.

Empire may well go to war, but it's out in the open now—too ugly to behold its own reflection. Too ugly even to rally its own people. It won't be long before the majority of American people become our allies.

In Washington, a quarter of a million people marched against the war on Iraq.[148] Each month, the protest is gathering momentum.

Arundhati Roy

Before September 11, 2001 America had a secret history. Secret especially from its own people. But now America's secrets are history, and its history is public knowledge. It's street talk.

Today, we know that every argument that is being used to escalate the war against Iraq is a lie. The most ludicrous of them being the U.S. government's deep commitment to bring democracy to Iraq.

Killing people to save them from dictatorship or ideological corruption is, of course, an old U.S. government sport. Here in Latin America, you know that better than most.

Nobody doubts that Saddam Hussein is a ruthless dictator, a murderer (whose worst excesses were supported by the governments of the United States and Great Britain). There's no doubt that Iraqis would be better off without him.

But, then, the whole world would be better off without a certain Mr. Bush. In fact, he is far more dangerous than Saddam Hussein.

So, should we bomb Bush out of the White House?

War Talk

It's more than clear that Bush is determined to go to war against Iraq, *regardless* of the facts—and regardless of international public opinion.

In its recruitment drive for allies, the United States is prepared to *invent* facts.

The charade with weapons inspectors is the U.S. government's offensive, insulting concession to some twisted form of international etiquette. It's like leaving the "doggie door" open for last minute "allies" or maybe the United Nations to crawl through.

But for all intents and purposes, the new war against Iraq has begun.

What can we do?

We can hone our memory, we can learn from our history. We can continue to build public opinion until it becomes a deafening roar.

We can turn the war on Iraq into a fishbowl of the U.S. government's excesses.

We can expose George Bush and Tony Blair—and their allies—for the cowardly baby killers, water poisoners, and pusillanimous long-distance bombers that they are.

We can re-invent civil disobedience in a million different ways. In other words, we can come up with a million ways of becoming a collective pain in the ass.

When George Bush says "You're either with us, or you are with the terrorists," we can say "No thank you." We can let him know that the people of the world do not need to choose between a Malevolent Mickey Mouse and the Mad Mullahs.

Our strategy should be not only to confront Empire, but to lay siege to it. To deprive it of oxygen. To shame it. To mock it. With our art, our music, our literature, our stubbornness, our joy, our brilliance, our sheer relentlessness—and our ability to tell our own stories. Stories that are different from the ones we're being brainwashed to believe.

The corporate revolution will collapse if we refuse to buy what they are selling—their ideas, their version of history, their wars, their weapons, their notion of inevitability.

Remember this: We be many and they be few. They need us more than we need them.

GLOSSARY

Adivasi: Tribal, but literally original, inhabitants of India.

Babri Masjid: On December 6, 1992, violent mobs of Hindu fundamentalists converged on the town of Ayodhya and demolished the Babri Masjid, an old Muslim mosque. Initiated by the BJP leader L.K. Advani, this was the culmination of a nationwide campaign to "arouse the pride" of Hindus. Plans for replacing it with a huge Hindu temple (Ram Mandir) are under way.

Bajrang Dal: Hindu nationalist organization tied to the Bharatiya Janata Party and linked, along with the Vishwa Hindu Parishad, to the destruction of the Babri Masjid in Ayodhya in 1992.

Bharatiya Janata Party (BJP): A Hindu nationalist party (literally, the Indian People's Party).

Dalit: Those who are oppressed or literally "ground down." The preferred term for those people who used to be called "untouchables" in India.

Dandi March: In March 1930, Gandhi and more than seventy other activists began a twenty-three day march to the coastal Indian village of Dandi, called the "salt march" because Gandhi called for the illegal production and purchase of salt by the native population. He called the march, widely considered a major turning point in the struggle for Independence, "the final struggle of freedom."

Dargah: Muslim tomb.

Hindutva: Philosophy seeking to strengthen "Hindu identity" and create a Hindu state, advocated by the BJP and other communalist parties.

Hydel: Hydroelectric power.

Madrassa: Muslim school.

Mandir: Temple.

Masjid: Mosque.

Narmada Bachao Andolan (NBA): Save the Narmada Movement.

Parsis: Persian-descended Zoroastrians.

Ram Mandir: See the glossary entry for Babri Masjid above.

Rashtriya Swayamsevak Sangh (RSS): Literally, the National Self-Help Group. A right-wing Hindu cultural guild with a clearly articulated anti-Muslim stand and a nationalistic notion of *hindutva*. The RSS is the ideological backbone of the BJP.

Saraswati shishu mandirs: Literally, Temples for Children, named after Saraswati, the Hindu goddess of learning.

Shakha: An RSS branch (literally) or center. RSS shakhas are "educational" cells.

Shiv Sena: A rabid right-wing regional Hindu chauvinist party in the State of Maharashtra.

Tehelka case: An exposé by the Tehelka web site, in which senior Indian politicians, defense officers, and government servants were secretly filmed accepting bribes from journalists posing as arms dealers.

NOTES

1 *Prophecy.* 16 mm. Nagasaki, Japan: Nagasaki Publishing Committee, 1982.

2 See Aruna Roy and Nikhil Dey, "Words and Deeds," India Together, June 2002, and "Stand-Off at Maan River: Dispossession Continues to Stalk the Narmada Valley," India Together, May 2002. Available on-line at http://www.indiatogether.org/campaigns/narmada/. See also "Maan Dam," Friends of River Narmada. Available on-line at http://www.narmada.org/nvdp.dams/maan/.

3 "Nobel laureate Amartya Sen may think that health and education are the reasons why India has lagged behind in development in the past 50 years, but I think it is because of defence," said Home Minister L.K. Advani. See "Quote of the Week, Other Voices," *India Today,* June 17, 2002, p. 13.

4 See Human Rights Watch, "Behind the Kashmir Conflict: Abuses by Indian Security Forces and Militant Groups Continue," 1999. Available on-line at http://www.hrw.org/reports/1999/kashmir/summary.htm.

5 See John Pilger, "Pakistan and India on Brink," *The Mirror* (London), May 27, 2002, p. 4. Neil Mackay, "Cash

from Chaos: How Britain Arms Both Sides," *The Sunday Herald* (Scotland), June 2, 2002, p. 12.

6   See Richard Norton-Taylor, "U.K. Is Selling Arms to India," *The Guardian* (London), June 20, 2002, p. 1. Tom Baldwin, Philip Webster, and Michael Evans, "Arms Export Row Damages Peace Mission," *The Times* (London), May 28, 2002. Agence France-Presse, "Blair Peace Shuttle Moves from India to Pakistan," January 7, 2002.

7   Pilger, "Pakistan and India on Brink," p. 4.

8   The government of India plans to build thirty large, 135 medium, and 3,000 small dams on the Narmada to generate electricity, displacing 400,000 people in the process. For more information, see http://www.narmada.org.

9   See http://www.jang.com.pk/thenews/spedition/pak-india/accord.htm.

10 The activists ended their fast on June 18, 2002 after an independent committee was set up to look into the issue of resettlement. For more information, see http://www.narmada.org/nba-press-releases;jun-2002/fast.ends.html.

11 Name changed.

12 Violence was directed especially at women. See, for example, the following report by Laxmi Murthy: "A doctor in rural Vadodara said that the wounded who started pouring in from February 28 had injuries of a kind he had never witnessed before even in earlier situations of communal violence. In a grave challenge to the Hippocratic oath, doctors have been threatened for treating Muslim patients, and pressurised to use the blood donated by RSS volunteers only to treat Hindu patients. Sword injuries, mutilated breasts and burns of

varying intensity characterised the early days of the massacre. Doctors conducted post-mortems on a number of women who had been gang raped, many of whom had been burnt subsequently. A woman from Kheda district who was gangraped had her head shaved and 'Om' cut into her head with a knife by the rapists. She died after a few days in the hospital. There were other instances of 'Om' engraved with a knife on women's backs and buttocks." From Laxmi Murthy, "In the Name of Honour," CorpWatch India, April 23, 2002. Available on-line at http://www.corpwatchindia.org/issues/PID.jsp?articleid=1283.

13 See "Stray Incidents Take Gujarat Toll to 544," *The Times of India,* March 5, 2002.

14 Edna Fernandes, "India Pushes Through Anti-Terror Law," *Financial Times* (London), March 27, 2002, p. 11; "Terror Law Gets President's Nod," *The Times of India,* April 3, 2002; Scott Baldauf, "As Spring Arrives, Kashmir Braces for Fresh Fighting," *Christian Science Monitor,* April 9, 2002, p. 7; Howard W. French and Raymond Bonner, "At Tense Time, Pakistan Starts to Test Missiles," *New York Times,* May 25, 2002, p. A1; Edward Luce, "The Saffron Revolution," *Financial Times* (London), May 4, 2002, p. 1; Martin Regg Cohn, "India's 'Saffron' Curriculum," *Toronto Star,* April 14, 2002, p. B4; and Pankaj Mishra, "Holy Lies," *The Guardian* (London), April 6, 2002, p. 24.

15 See Edward Luce, "Battle Over Ayodhya Temple Looms," *Financial Times* (London), February 2, 2002, p. 7.

16 "Gujarat's Tale of Sorrow: 846 Dead," *The Economic Times,* April 18, 2002; See also Celia W. Dugger, "Religious Riots

Loom Over Indian Politics," *New York Times,* July 27, 2002, p. A1; and Edna Fernandes, "Gujarat Violence Backed by State, Says EU Report," *Financial Times* (London), April 30, 2002, p. 12. See also Human Rights Watch, "'We Have No Orders To Save You': State Participation and Complicity in Communal Violence in Gujarat," Vol. 14, No. 3(C), April 2002 [hereafter: "HRW Report"]. Available on-line at http://www.hrw.org/reports/2002/india/ and in PDF format at http://hrw.org/reports/2002/india/gujarat.pdf. See also Human Rights Watch, Press Release, "India: Gujarat Officials Took Part in Anti-Muslim Violence," New York, April 30, 2002.

17 "A Tainted Election," *Indian Express,* April 17, 2002; and Meena Menon, "A Divided Gujarat Not Ready for Snap Poll," Inter Press Service, July 21, 2002.

18 See HRW Report, pp. 27–31. Dugger, "Religious Riots Loom Over Indian Politics," p. A1; "Women Relive the Horrors of Gujarat," *The Hindu,* May 18, 2002; Harbaksh Singh Nanda, "Muslim Survivors Speak in India," United Press International, April 27, 2002; and "Gujarat Carnage: The Aftermath: Impact of Violence on Women," 2002, OnlineVolunteers.org. Available on-line at http://www.onlinevolunteers.org/gujarat/women/index.htm.

19 HRW Report, pp. 15–16, 31; and Justice A.P. Ravani, Submission to the National Human Rights Commission, New Delhi, March 21, 2002, Appendix 4. Available on-line at http://www.secularindia.com/13new.htm. See also Dugger, "Religious Riots Loom Over Indian Politics," p. A1.

20   HRW Report, p. 31; and "Artists Protest Destruction of Cultural Landmarks," Press Trust of India, April 13, 2002.

21   HRW Report, pp. 7, 45. Rama Lakshmi, "Sectarian Violence Haunts Indian City: Hindu Militants Bar Muslims from Work," *Washington Post,* April 8, 2002, p. A12.

22   *Communalism Combat* (March–April 2002) recounted Jaffri's final moments: "Ehsan Jaffri is pulled out of his house, brutally treated for 45 minutes, stripped, paraded naked, and asked to say, 'Vande Maataram!' and 'Jai Shri Ram!' He refuses. His fingers are chopped off, he is paraded around in the locality, badly injured. Next, his hands and feet are chopped off. He is then dragged, a fork-like instrument clutching his neck, down the road before being thrown into the fire." See also "50 Killed in Communal Violence in Gujarat, 30 of Them Burnt," Press Trust of India, February 28, 2002.

23   HRW Report, p. 5. See also Dugger, "Religious Riots Loom Over Indian Politics," p. A1.

24   "ML Launches Frontal Attack on Sangh Parivar," *The Times of India,* May 8, 2002.

25   HRW Report, pp. 21–27. See also the remarks of Kamal Mitra Chenoy of Jawaharlal Nehru University, who led an independent fact-finding mission to Gujarat, "Can India End Religious Revenge?" CNN International, "Q&A with Zain Verjee," April 4, 2002.

26   See Tavleen Sigh, "Out of Tune," *India Today,* April 15, 2002, p. 21. See also Sharad Gupta, "BJP: His Excellency," *India Today,* January 28, 2002, p. 18.

27   Khozem Merchant, "Gujarat: Vajpayee Visits Scene of Communal Clashes," *Financial Times* (London), April 5,

2002, p. 10. See also Pushpesh Pant, "Atal at the Helm, or Running on Auto?" *The Times of India,* April 8, 2002.

28   See Bharat Desai, "Will Vajpayee See Through All the Window Dressing?" *The Economic Times,* April 5, 2002.

29   Agence France-Press, "Singapore, India to Explore Closer Economic Ties," April 8, 2002.

30   See "Medha Files Charges Against BJP Leaders," *The Economic Times,* April 13, 2002.

31   HRW Report, p. 30. See also Burhan Wazir, "Militants Seek Muslim-Free India," *The Observer* (London), July 21, 2002, p. 20.

32   See Mishra, "Holy Lies," p. 24.

33   The Home Minister, L.K Advani, made a public statement claiming that the burning of the train was a plot by Pakistan's Inter Services Intelligence (ISI). Months later, the police have not found a shred of evidence to support that claim. The Gujarat government's forensic report says that sixty liters of petrol were poured onto the floor by someone who was inside the carriage. The doors were locked, possibly from the inside. The burned bodies of the passengers were found in a heap in the middle of the carriage. So far, nobody knows who started the fire. There are theories to suit every political position: It was a Pakistani plot. It was Muslim extremists who managed to get into the train. It was the angry mob. It was a VHP/Bajrang Dal plot staged to set off the horror that followed. No one really knows. See HRW Report, pp. 13–14; Siddharth Srivastava, "No Proof Yet on ISI Link with Sabarmati Attack: Officials," *The Times of India,* March 6, 2002; "ISI Behind Godhra Killings, Says BJP," *The Times of India,* March 18, 2002; Uday Mahurkar, "Gujarat:

Fuelling The Fire," *India Today,* July 22, 2002, p. 38;
"Bloodstained Memories," *Indian Express,* April 12, 2002;
and Celia W. Dugger, "After Deadly Firestorm, India
Officials Ask Why," *New York Times,* March 6, 2002, p. A3.

34   "Blame it on Newton's Law: Modi," *The Times of India,*
March 3, 2002. See also Fernandes, "Gujarat Violence
Backed by State," p. 12.

35   "RSS Cautions Muslims," Press Trust of India, March
17, 2002. See also Sanghamitra Chakraborty, "Minority
Guide to Good Behaviour," *The Times of India,* March 25,
2002. The full text of the resolution ("Resolution 3:
Godhra and After") is available on-line at
http://www.rss.org/reso2002.htm.

36   P.R. Ramesh, "Modi Offers to Quit as Gujarat CM," *The
Economic Times,* April 13, 2002. "Modi Asked to Seek
Mandate," *The Statesman* (India), April 13, 2002.

37   See M.S. Golwalkar, *We, or Our Nationhood Defined*
(Nagpur: Bharat Publications, 1939), and Vinayak
Damodar Savarkar, *Hindutva* (New Delhi: Bharti Sadan,
1989). See also Editorial, "Saffron Is Thicker Than …,"
The Hindu, October 22, 2000; and David Gardner,
"Hindu Revivalists Raise the Question of Who Governs
India," *Financial Times* (London), July 13, 2000, p. 12.

38   See Arundhati Roy, *Power Politics,* 2nd ed. (Cambridge:
South End Press, 2001), p. 57 and notes (p. 159).

39   See Noam Chomsky, "Militarizing Space 'To Protect
U.S. Interests and Investment,'" *International Socialist
Review* 19 (July–August 2001). Available on-line at
http://www.isreview.org/issues/19/NoamChomsky.
shtml.

40 Pankaj Mishra, "A Mediocre Goddess," *New Statesman,* April 9, 2001, a review of Katherine Frank, *Indira: A Life of Indira Nehru Gandhi* (London: HarperCollins, 2001).

41 William Claiborne, "Gandhi Urges Indians to Strengthen Union," *Washington Post,* November 20, 1984, p. A9. See also Tavleen Singh, "Yesterday, Today, Tomorrow," *India Today,* March 30, 1998, p. 24.

42 HRW Report, pp. 39–44.

43 President George W. Bush, Address to Joint Session of Congress, "September 11, 2001, Terrorist Attacks on the United States," Federal News Service, September 20, 2001.

44 Pilger, "Pakistan and India on Brink," p. 4.

45 Alison Leigh Cowan, Kurt Eichenwald, and Michael Moss, "Bin Laden Family, With Deep Western Ties, Strives to Re-establish a Name," *New York Times,* October 28, 2001, p. 1: 9.

46 Sanjeev Miglani, "Opposition Keeps Up Heat on Government Over Riots," Reuters, April 16, 2002.

47 "Either Govern or Just Go," *Indian Express,* April 1, 2002. Parekh is CEO of HDFC, the Housing Development Finance Corporation Limited.

48 "It's War in Drawing Rooms," *Indian Express,* May 19, 2002.

49 Ranjit Devraj, "Pro-Hindu Ruling Party Back to Hardline Politics," Inter Press Service, July 1, 2002; and "An Unholy Alliance," *Indian Express,* May 6, 2002.

50 Nilanjana Bhaduri Jha, "Congress [Party] Begins Oust-Modi Campaign," *The Economic Times,* April 12, 2002.

51 Richard Benedetto, "Confidence in War on Terror Wanes," *USA Today,* June 25, 2002, p. 19A; and David Lamb, "Israel's Invasions, 20 Years Apart, Look Eerily Alike," *Los Angeles Times,* April 20, 2002, p. A5.

52 See Arundhati Roy, "The End of Imagination," in *The Cost of Living* (New York: Modern Library, 1999).

53 "I would say it is a weapon of peace guarantee, a peace guarantor," said Abdul Qadeer Khan of Pakistan's nuclear bomb. See Imtiaz Gul, "Father of Pakistani Bomb Says Nuclear Weapons Guarantee Peace," Deutsche Presse-Agentur, May 29, 1998. See also Raj Chengappa, *Weapons of Peace: The Secret Story of India's Quest to Be a Nuclear Power* (New Delhi: HarperCollins, 2000).

54 The 1999 Kargil war between India and Pakistan claimed hundreds of lives. See Edward Luce, "Fernandes Hit by India's Coffin Scandal," *Financial Times* (London), December 13, 2001, p. 12.

55 See "Arrested Growth," *The Times of India,* February 2, 2000.

56 Dugger, "Religious Riots Loom Over Indian Politics," p. A1.

57 Edna Fernandes, "EU Tells India of Concern Over Violence in Gujarat," *Financial Times* (London), May 3, 2002, p. 12; and Alex Spillius, "'Please Don't Say This Was a Riot. It Was Genocide, Pure and Simple,'" *The Daily Telegraph* (London), June 18, 2002, p. 13.

58 "Gujarat is an internal matter and the situation is under control," said Jaswant Singh, India's foreign affairs minister. See Shishir Gupta, "The Foreign Hand," *India Today,* May 6, 2002, p. 42, and sidebar.

59 "Laloo Wants Use of POTA [Prevention of Terrorism Act] Against VHP, RSS," *The Times of India,* March 7, 2002.

60 See John Berger, *G.* (New York: Vintage International, 1991).

61   See Damon Johnston, "U.S. Hits Back Inspirations," *The Advertiser,* September 22, 2001, p. 7.

62   See John Pomfret, "Chinese Working Overtime to Sew U.S. Flags," *Washington Post,* September 20, 2001, p. A14.

63   See "Democracy: Who Is She When She's at Home?" pp. 17–44 above.

64   See David E. Sanger, "Bin Laden Is Wanted in Attacks, 'Dead or Alive,' President Says," *New York Times,* September 18, 2001, p. A1; and John F. Burns, "10-Month Afghan Mystery: Is bin Laden Dead or Alive?" *New York Times,* September 30, 2002, p. A1.

65   See the Associated Press database of those confirmed dead, reported dead, or reported missing in the September 11 terrorist attacks (http://attacksvictims.ap.org/totals.asp).

66   Quoted in Seymour M. Hersh, *The Price of Power: Kissinger in the Nixon White House* (New York: Summit Books, 1983), p. 265.

67   See *Chile: The Other September 11,* eds. Pilar Aguilera and Ricardo Fredes (New York: Ocean Press, 2002); Amnesty International, "The Case of Augusto Pinochet" (http://www.amnestyusa.org/countries/chile/pinochet _case.html).

68   Clifford Krauss, "Britain Arrests Pinochet to Face Charges by Spain," *New York Times,* October 18, 1998, p. 1: 1; National Security Archive, "Chile: 16,000 Secret U.S. Documents Declassified," Press Release, November 13, 2000 (http://www.gwu.edu/~nsarchiv/news/ 20001113/); and selected documents on the National Security Archive website (http://www.gwu.edu/ ~nsarchiv/news/20001113/#docs).

69 Kissinger told this to Pinochet at a meeting of the Organization of American States in Santiago, Chile, on June 8, 1976. See Lucy Kosimar, "Kissinger Covered Up Chile Torture," *The Observer,* February 28, 1999, p. 3.

70 Among other histories, see Eduardo Galeano, *Open Veins of Latin America: Five Centuries of the Pillage of a Continent,* 2nd ed., trans. Cedric Belfrage (New York: Monthly Review Press, 1998); Noam Chomsky, *Turning the Tide: U.S. Intervention in Central America and the Struggle for Peace,* 2nd ed. (Boston: South End Press, 1985); Noam Chomsky, *The Culture of Terrorism* (Boston: South End Press, 1983); and Gabriel Kolko, *Confronting the Third World: United States Foreign Policy, 1945–1980* (New York: Pantheon, 1988).

71 In a public relations move, the SOA renamed itself the Western Hemisphere Institute for Security Cooperation (WHISC) on January 17, 2001. See Jack Nelson-Pallmeyer, *School of Assassins: Guns, Greed, and Globalization,* 2nd ed. (New York: Orbis Books, 2001); Michael Gormley, "Army School Faces Critics Who Call It Training Ground for Assassins," Associated Press, May 2, 1998; and School of the Americas Watch (http://www.soaw.org).

72 On these interventions, see, among other sources, Noam Chomsky, *American Power and the New Mandarins,* 2nd ed. (New York: New Press, 2002); Noam Chomsky, *At War With Asia* (New York: Vintage Books, 1970); and Howard Zinn, *Vietnam: The Logic Of Withdrawal,* 2nd ed. (Cambridge: South End Press, 2002).

73 See Samih K. Farsoun and Christina E. Zacharia, *Palestine and the Palestinians* (Boulder, Colorado: Westview Press, 1997), p. 10.

74 The Balfour Declaration is included in Farsoun and Zacharia, *Palestine and the Palestinians,* Appendix 2, p. 320.

75 Quoted in Noam Chomsky, *Fateful Triangle: The United States, Israel, and the Palestinians,* 2nd ed. (Cambridge: South End Press, 2000), p. 90.

76 Quoted in Editorial, "Scurrying Towards Bethlehem," *New Left Review* 10, 2nd series (July/August 2001), p. 9, n. 5.

77 Quoted in Farsoun and Zacharia, *Palestine and the Palestinians,* pp. 10 and 243.

78 Farsoun and Zacharia, *Palestine and the Palestinians,* pp. 111 and 123.

79 Farsoun and Zacharia, *Palestine and the Palestinians,* p. 116.

80 See Chomsky, *Fateful Triangle,* pp. 103–107, 118–32, and 156–60.

81 From 1987 to 2002, alone, more than 2,000 Palestinians were killed. See B'Tselem (The Israeli Information Center for Human Rights in the Occupied Territories), "Palestinians Killed in the Occupied Territories," Table (http://www.btselem.org/English/Statistics/Total_ Casualties.asp).

82 See Naseer H. Aruri, *Dishonest Broker: The United States, Israel, and the Palestinians* (Cambridge: South End Press, 2003); Noam Chomsky, *World Orders Old and New,* 2nd ed. (New York: Columbia University Press, 1996).

83 In addition to more than $3 billion annually in official Foreign Military Financing, the U.S. government supplies Israel with economic assistance, loans, technology transfers, and arms sales. See Nick Anderson, "House Panel Increases Aid for Israel, Palestinians," *Los Angeles Times,* May 10, 2002, p. A1; See Aruri, *Dishonest Broker;* and Anthony Arnove and Ahmed Shawki,

Foreword, *The Struggle for Palestine,* ed. Lance Selfa (Chicago: Haymarket Books, 2002), p. xxv.

84 Article 27 of the Charter of the Islamic Resistance Movement (Hamas), quoted in Farsoun and Zacharia, *Palestine and the Palestinians,* Appendix 13, p. 339.

85 George W. Bush, "Text of Bush's Speech: 'It Is Iraq Against the World,'" *Los Angeles Times,* September 12, 1990, p. A7.

86 See Glenn Frankel, "Iraq Long Avoided Censure on Rights," *Washington Post,* September 22, 1990, p. A1.

87 See Christopher Dickey and Evan Thomas, "How Saddam Happened," *Newsweek,* September 23, 2002, pp. 35–37.

88 See Anthony Arnove, Introduction, *Iraq Under Siege: The Deadly Impact of Sanctions and War,* 2nd ed., ed. Anthony Arnove (Cambridge: South End Press; London: Pluto Press, 2002), p. 20.

89 See Arnove, *Iraq Under Siege,* pp. 221–22.

90 See Arnove, *Iraq Under Siege,* pp. 17, 205.

91 See Thomas J. Nagy, "The Secret Behind the Sanctions: How the U.S. Intentionally Destroyed Iraq's Water Supply," *The Progressive* 65: 9 (September 2001).

92 See Arnove, *Iraq Under Siege,* pp. 121 and 185–203. See also Nicholas D. Kristof, "The Stones of Baghdad," *New York Times,* October 4, 2002, p. A27.

93 Leslie Stahl, "Punishing Saddam," produced by Catherine Olian, CBS, *60 Minutes,* May 12, 1996.

94 Elisabeth Bumiller, "Bush Aides Set Strategy to Sell Policy on Iraq," *New York Times,* September 7, 2002, p. A1.

95 Richard Perle, "Why the West Must Strike First Against Saddam Hussein," *Daily Telegraph* (London), August 9, 2002, p. 22.

96 See Alan Simpson and Glen Rangwala, "The Dishonest Case for a War on Iraq," September 27, 2002 (http://www.traprockpeace.org/counter-dossier.html) and Glen Rangwala, "Notes Further to the Counter-Dossier," September 29, 2002 (http://www.traprockpeace.org/counter-dossier.html #notes).

97 George Bush, "Bush's Remarks on U.S. Military Strikes in Afghanistan," *New York Times,* October 8, 2001, p. B6.

98 See Paul Watson, "Afghanistan Aims to Revive Pipeline Plans," *Los Angeles Times,* May 30, 2002, p. A1; and Ilene R. Prusher, Scott Baldauf, and Edward Girardet, "Afghan Power Brokers," *Christian Science Monitor,* June 10, 2002, p. 1.

99 See Lisa Fingeret et al., "Markets Worry That Conflict Could Spread in Area That Holds Two-Thirds of World Reserves," *Financial Times* (London), April 2, 2002, p. 1.

100 Thomas L. Friedman, "Craziness Pays," *New York Times,* February 24, 1998, p. A21.

101 Thomas L. Friedman, *The Lexus and the Olive Tree: Understanding Globalization* (New York: Farrar, Strauss, and Giroux, 1999), p. 373.

102 Statistics from Joseph E. Stiglitz, *Globalization and Its Discontents* (New York and London: W.W. Norton, 2002), p. 5; Noam Chomsky, *Rogue States: The Rule of Law in World Affairs* (Cambridge: South End Press, 2000), p. 214; and Noreena Hertz, "Why Consumer Power Is Not Enough," *New Statesman,* April 30, 2001.

103 Among the many treaties and international agreements the United States has not signed, ignores, violates, or has broken are: the UN International Covenant on Economic, Social and Cultural Rights (1966); the UN Convention on the Rights of the Child (CRC); the UN Convention on the Elimination of All Forms of Discrimination Against Women (CEDAW); agreements setting the jurisdiction for the International Criminal Court (ICC); the 1972 Anti-Ballistic Missile Treaty with Russia; the Comprehensive Test Ban Treaty (CTBT); and the Kyoto Protocol regulating greenhouse gas emissions.

104 See David Cole and James X. Dempsey, *Terrorism and the Constitution: Sacrificing Civil Liberties in the Name of National Security* (New York: New Press, 2002).

105 Luke Harding, "Elusive Mullah Omar 'Back in Afghanistan,'" *Guardian* (London), August 30, 2002, p. 12.

106 See Human Rights Watch, "Opportunism in the Face of Tragedy: Repression in the Name of Anti-Terrorism" (http://www.hrw.org/campaigns/september11/opportunismwatch.htm).

107 See Arundhati Roy, *Power Politics*, pp. 119–20 and notes (p. 170).

108 R.W. Apple, Jr., "Bush Appears in Trouble Despite Two Big Advantages," *New York Times,* August 4, 1988, p. A1. Bush made this remark in refusing to apologize for the shooting down of an Iranian passenger plane, killing 290 passengers. See Lewis Lapham, *Theater of War* (New York: New Press, 2002), p. 126.

109 Chomsky would be the first to point out that other pioneering media analysts include his frequent co-author, Edward Herman, Ben Bagdikian (whose 1983 classic *The*

Media Monopoly recounts the suppression of Chomsky and Herman's *Counter-Revolutionary Violence: Bloodbaths in Fact and Propaganda*), and Herbert Schiller.

110 Paul Betts, "Ciampi Calls for Review of Media Laws," *Financial Times* (London), July 24, 2002, p. 8. For an overview of Berlusconi's holdings, see Ketupa.net Media Profiles: http://www.ketupa.net/berlusconi1.htm.

111 See Sabin Russell, "U.S. Push for Cheap Cipro Haunts AIDS Drug Dispute," *San Francisco Chronicle,* November 8, 2001, p. A13; Frank Swoboda and Martha McNeil Hamilton, "Congress Passes \$15 Billion Airline Bailout," *Washington Post,* September 22, 2001, p. A1.

112 President George W. Bush Jr., "President Bush's Address on Terrorism Before a Joint Meeting of Congress," *New York Times,* September 21, 2001, p. B4.

113 Dan Eggen, "Ashcroft Invokes Religion in U.S. War on Terrorism," *Washington Post,* February 20, 2002, p. A2.

114 President George W. Bush Jr., "Bush's Remarks on U.S. Military Strikes in Afghanistan," *New York Times,* October 8, 2001, p. B6.

115 President George W. Bush Jr., Remarks at FBI Headquarters, Washington, D.C., October 10, 2001, Federal Document Clearinghouse.

116 See Howard Zinn, *A People's History of the United States: 1492–Present,* 20th anniversary edition (New York: HarperCollins, 2001).

117 Bob Marley and N.G. Williams (*aka* King Sporty), "Buffalo Soldier."

118 Noam Chomsky, "The Manufacture of Consent," in *The Chomsky Reader,* ed. James Peck (New York: Pantheon, 1987), pp. 121–22.

119 See Jim Miller, "Report From the Inferno," *Newsweek,* September 7, 1981, p. 72, review of Committee for the Compilation of Materials on Damage Caused by the Atomic Bombs in Hiroshima and Nagasaki, *Hiroshima and Nagasaki: The Physical, Medical, and Social Effects of the Atomic Bombings* (New York: Basic, 1981).

120 David E. Sanger, "Bush to Formalize a Defense Policy of Hitting First," *New York Times,* June 17, 2002, p. A1; David E. Sanger, "Bush Renews Pledge to Strike First to Counter Terror Threats," *New York Times,* July 20, 2002, p. A3. See also *The National Security Strategy of the United States of America,* September 20, 2002: http://www.whitehouse.gov/nsc/nss.html.

121 See Terence O'Malley, "The Afghan Memory Holds Little Room for Trust in U.S.," *Irish Times,* October 15, 2001, p. 16.

122 Arnove, ed., *Iraq Under Siege.*

123 See Noam Chomsky, "Memories," review of *In Retrospect* by Robert McNamara (New York: Times Books, 1995), in *Z Magazine* (July–August 1995). Available online at http://www.zmag.org/.

124 "Myth and Reality in Bloody Battle for the Skies," *Guardian* (London), October 13, 1998, p. 15.

125 Bill Keller, "Moscow Says Afghan Role Was Illegal and Immoral," *New York Times,* October 24, 1989, p. A1.

126 Noam Chomsky, "Afghanistan and South Vietnam," in *The Chomsky Reader,* ed. Peck, p. 225.

127 Samuel P. Huntington, "The Bases of Accommodation," *Foreign Affairs* 46: 4 (1968): 642–56. Quoted in Noam Chomsky, *At War with Asia* (New York: Vintage Books, 1970), p. 87.

128 Samuel P. Huntington, "The Clash of Civilizations?" *Foreign Affairs* 72: 3 (Summer 1993): 22–49.

129 Huntington, "The Bases of Accommodation." Quoted in Chomsky, *At War with Asia*, p. 87.

130 T. D. Allman, "The Blind Bombers," *Far Eastern Economic Review* 75: 5 (January 29, 1972): 18–20. Quoted in Noam Chomsky, *For Reasons of State* (New York: New Press, 2003), p. 72.

131 Chomsky, *For Reasons of State,* p. 72; Chomsky, *At War with Asia,* p. 87; and Lapham, *Theater of War,* p. 145.

132 T. D. Allman, "The War in Laos: Plain Facts," *Far Eastern Economic Review* 75: 2 (January 8, 1972): 16ff.

133 Chomsky, *For Reasons of State,* p. 18. See also Noam Chomsky, "The Pentagon Papers as Propaganda and as History," in Noam Chomsky and Howard Zinn, ed., *The Pentagon Papers: The Defense Department History of United States Decisionmaking on Vietnam: The Senator Gravel Edition: Critical Essays* (Boston: Beacon Press, 1971–72), vol. 5, pp. 79–201.

134 Chomsky, *For Reasons of State,* pp. 67 and 70.

135 William Pfaff, *Condemned to Freedom: The Breakdown of Liberal Society* (New York: Random House, 1971), pp. 75–77. Quoted in Chomsky, *For Reasons of State,* p. 94.

136 Pfaff, *Condemned to Freedom,* pp. 75–77. Chomsky, *For Reasons of State,* pp. 94–95.

137 *The Pentagon Papers,* vol. 4, p. 43. Quoted in Chomsky, *For Reasons of State,* p. 67.

138 Philip Jones Griffiths, *Vietnam Inc.,* 2nd ed. (New York: Phaidon, 2001), p. 210. First edition quoted in Chomsky, *For Reasons of State,* pp. 3–4.

139 Noam Chomsky, interview with James Peck, in *The Chomsky Reader,* ed. Peck, p. 14.

140 See Ranjit Devraj, "Asia's 'Outcast' Hurt By Globalization," Inter Press Service, January 6, 2003; Statesman News Service, "Farm Suicide Heat on Jaya," *The Statesman* (India), January 9, 2003; and " 'Govt. Policies Driving Farmers to Suicide,'" *The Times of India,* February 4, 2002.

141 See "Govt.'s Food Policy Gets a Reality Check from States," *Indian Express,* January 11, 2003; and Parul Chandra, "Victims Speak of Hunger, Starvation Across Country," *The Times of India,* January 11, 2003.

142 See "Democracy: Who Is She When She's at Home?" pp. 17–44 above; See also Pankaj Mishra, "The Other Face of Fanaticism," *New York Times,* February 2, 2003, pp. 6: 42–46; and Concerned Citizens Tribunal, *Crime Against Humanity: An Inquiry Into the Carnage in Gujarat,* 2 vols. (Mumbai, India: Citizens for Justice and Peace, 2002).

143 See Edward Luce, "Gujarat Win Likely to Embolden Hindu Right," *Financial Times* (London), December 16, 2002, p. 8.

144 See Oscar Olivera, "The War Over Water in Cochabamba, Bolivia," trans. Florencia Belvedere, presented at "Services for All?" Municipal Services Project (MSP) Conference, South Africa, May 15–18, 2002, http://qsilver.queensu.ca/~mspadmin/pages/Conferences/Services/Olivera.htm.

145 See Tom Lewis, "Contagion in Latin America," *International Socialist Review* 24 (July–August 2002).

146 See Julian Borger and Alex Bellos, "U.S. 'Gave the Nod' to Venezuelan Coup," *Guardian* (London), April 17, 2002, p. 13.

147 See David Sharrock, "Thousands Protest in Buenos Aires as Economic Woes Persist," *The Times* (London), December 21, 2002, p. 18.

148 See Mary McGrory, "'A River of Peaceful People,'" *Washington Post,* January 23, 2003, p. A21.

INDEX

pogrom

resistance movements: around
the world, 71, 108–12; in
India, 3–4, 6, 9–13, 38,
116n10; nonviolence of, 14.
See also Narmada Bachao
Andolan

RSS. *See* Rashtriya Swayamsevak
Sangh

Rumsfeld, Donald, 74

Russia, 75, 90–91, 99

S

Sabarmati Express. *See* Godhra
train burning

Said, Edward, 49

Sangh Parivar, 25–28, 36

Saudi Arabia, 51

Save the Narmada Movement. *See*
Narmada Bachao Andolan

Schiller, Herbert, 129n109

School of the Americas (SOA),
55, 125n71

Sen, Amartya, 4–5, 115n3

September 11th: Bush on, 81–82;
changes since, 69, 109–10;
losses, 52–53, 88, 124n65;
media response to, 79; Middle
East and, 62–63

Shamir, Yitzhak, 59

Sharon, Ariel, 34

Shiv Sena, 30

Sikhs, 27

Singh, Digvijay, 15

Singh, Jaswant, 25, 123n58

slavery, 85–86

South America, 53–56

South Vietnam, 90–92, 96

starvation, 97, 105

state: citizen relationship to,
37–38, 47–52, 82;
globalization supported by, 72;
pogroms and, 5, 23–24, 29, 43;
terrorism by, 49–50. *See also*
nationalism

structural adjustment programs.
See globalization

suicide bombing, 60–62

suicide by farmers, 104–5

T

Taliban, 28, 51, 73

terrorism: alternatives to, 13, 15;
globalization and, 71, 103;
logic of, 82; by the state,
23–24, 29, 43, 49–50; suicide
bombing, 60–62. *See also*
September 11th; War Against
Terrorism

Thackeray, Bal, 30

Truman, Harry, 88

Turkey, 64

U

United Kingdom. *See* Britain

United Nations, 59, 61, 69, 111

United States: Afghanistan
bombed by, 30, 50–51, 73, 85;
arms dealing by, 30, 61, 63–64;
citizenship vs. nationalism in,
48–52; criticism of, 83;
cynicism about, 31; founding

of, 86–87; imperialism of,
69–70, 74–75, 83–87, 89–90,
101, 103, 129n103; Iraq war,
52, 63–69, 88, 109–11; Israel
supported by, 61, 126n83;
Latin American imperialism
by, 53–56; loss of freedom in,
73; media in, 79; militarism of,
68, 97; nuclear weapons and,
2–3, 56–57, 67, 84, 88–89;
resistance movements in, 48,
109; unsustainability of, 74;
Venezuela and, 108; during
World War II, 56–57, 87–89.
See also Vietnam War
untouchables. *See* Dalits
USSR, 75, 90–91, 99
Uttar Pradesh, India, 32

V

Vajpayee, A.B.: alliances of, 24,
26; bigotry by, 31; during
Gujarat pogrom, 17–18, 21,
106
Venezuela, 108
Verma, Mangat, 10–12
Vietnam War: damage caused by,
91–95, 98; end of, 48; start of,
90–91; strategy of, 91–92,
95–99
violence vs. nonviolence, 13–15
Vishwa Hindu Parishad (VHP),
19–21, 25–26, 33

W

war: arms industry, 6, 30, 61,

63–64, 79; civil war potential
in India, 30–31, 43; critique of,
4–5, 52; against Iraq, 52,
63–69, 88, 109–11; U.S. and,
68–69, 97; Vietnam, 48,
90–99; World War II, 25,
43–44, 87–88. *See also*
Afghanistan; nuclear weapons;
Pakistan-India conflict
War Against Terrorism: Bush's
rhetoric on, 30, 46–47, 50–51,
81–82, 111; civil liberties lost,
73; covert actions behind,
108–9; critique of, 4, 6, 34;
imperialism in, 69–70;
patriotism in, 46–48;
unsustainability of U.S., 74
water systems. *See* dams
Western Hemisphere Institute for
Security Cooperation
(WHISC), 55, 125n71
women, 51, 19, 28, 105, 116n12
World Bank, 74–75, 103
WorldCom, 108
World Trade Organization,
74–75, 103–4
World War II, 25, 43–44, 87–88

Y

Yadav, Laloo, 43–44

Z

Zinn, Howard, 49
Zionism. *See* Israel

ABOUT ARUNDHATI ROY

Arundhati Roy is the author of the novel *The God of Small Things*, for which she was awarded the Booker Prize in 1997, and two previous essay collections: *Power Politics* (South End Press, 2001) and *The Cost of Living*. Roy

Photo © Pradip Krishen

received the 2002 Lannan Award for Cultural Freedom from the Lannan Foundation. Roy was trained as an architect. She lives in New Delhi, India.

ABOUT SOUTH END PRESS

South End Press is a nonprofit, collectively run book publisher with more than 200 titles in print. Since our founding in 1977, we have tried to meet the needs of readers who are exploring, or are already committed to, the politics of radical social change. Our goal is to publish books that encourage critical thinking and constructive action on the key political, cultural, social, economic, and ecological issues shaping life in the United States and in the world. In this way, we hope to give expression to a wide diversity of democratic social movements and to provide an alternative to the products of corporate publishing.

Through the Institute for Social and Cultural Change, South End Press works with other political media projects—Alternative Radio; Speakout, a speakers' bureau; and *Z Magazine*—to expand access to information and critical analysis.

Write or e-mail southend@southendpress.org for a free catalog, or visit www.southendpress.org.